Conscience and Conflict

A Trilogy of One-Actor Plays:

Thomas Merton
Pope John XXIII
Martin Luther

Anthony T. Padovano

Paulist Press / New York / Mahwah

Text design by Ellen Whitney

Library of Congress Cataloging-in-Publication Data

Padovano, Anthony T.
    Conscience and conflict : a trilogy of one-actor plays : Thomas Merton, Pope John XXIII, Martin Luther / Anthony T. Padovano.
        p.   cm.
    Contents: Winter rain — His name is John — Summer lightning.
    ISBN 0-8091-3001-7 (pbk.)
    1. Clergy—Drama. 2. Monodramas. 3. Merton, Thomas, 1915–1968, in fiction, drama, poetry, etc. 4. John XXIII, Pope, 1881–1963—Drama. 5. Luther, Martin, 1483–1546—Drama. I. Title.
PS3566.A3315C66   1988
812'.54—dc19   88-19492
                                                                     CIP

Published by Paulist Press
997 Macarthur Boulevard
Mahwah, NJ 07430

Printed and bound in the
United States of America

Contents

Introduction 1

Winter Rain 9

His Name Is John 37

Summer Lightning 67

Thomas Merton (1915–1968)

When Thomas Merton died, at the age of fifty-three, he had lived half of his life as a monk of the Abbey of Gethsemani (Kentucky). It is ironic that his fame is based on this latter half of his life, a time when he made efforts by silence, cloister and hermitage, to escape the world's notice. But, then, the career of Merton is one of contradictions and unexpected reversals.

Merton was born on January 31, 1915 in Prades, France, the first of two children of artist Owen Merton of Christchurch, New Zealand and of artist Ruth Jenkins Merton of Zanesville, Ohio. The family moved to New York City the next year to escape the ravages of World War I.

The loss of Thomas' mother while he was very young, of his father when he was sixteen, and of his younger brother in World War II, contributed to Merton's sense of the contingency of human life and, possibly, to his decision to enter monastic life. The influence from two parents who were artists and instinctive pacifists bore fruit in their son's pursuits as writer, poet, and prophet of non-violence.

The basic elements which influenced his later life were set in place during this period. They are dealt with in the first scene of *Winter Rain*.

Merton attended schools in the United States, Bermuda, France and England before commencing higher education. He entered Clare College of Cambridge University on scholarship and completed his undergraduate education at Columbia University in New York.

Merton's friendship with Professor Mark Van Doren, the Pulitzer-Prize poet, and fellow student Robert Lax, the future poet, developed his existing interests in mysticism, poetry and monasticism. He became a Roman Catholic in 1938, completed an M.A. in literature from Columbia in 1939, and entered the Abbey of Gethsemani in 1941 while working on a never-completed Ph.D. thesis on Gerard Manley Hopkins and teaching English at St. Bonaventure University in New York State.

A second phase of Merton's career begins with his life as a monk of the Cistercian Order of the Strict Observance. The rigor of this life (perpetual silence, vegetarian diet, hours at prayer) had as its purpose the development of contemplation. Many of those who knew Merton well believe he became a mystic during these years. This period is covered in the second scene of *Winter Rain*.

The last three years of Merton's life were lived as a hermit, formally connected to the monastery but removed from its activities. Scene four of *Winter Rain* occurs in the hermitage.

A further aspect of Merton's life involves him in writing, social protest, and Asian spirituality. The most widely known of his sixty books is *The Seven Storey Mountain*, an autobiography about his intense search for a life of meaning. The writings of Merton include eight volumes of poetry and some six hundred articles.

Merton's social protest was startling and unconventional. He objected vehemently to the U.S. involvement in the Vietnam War, the nuclear arms race, and violations of the human and civil rights of black Americans. This protest caused him difficulty at times with readers who believed monks should not voice their opinions on such matters. Church superiors reacted, on occasion, by denying him the right to publish.

In the final years, Merton was committed to Hindu and Buddhist spiritual wisdom as an integrating dimension of his Catholic Christianity. The conversation with Dr. D.T. Suzuki in scene three of *Winter Rain* explores this theme.

Zen Buddhism had a special attraction for Merton because of its emphasis on experience rather than doctrine.

Merton's personal journey was not always in the direction of certitude. In this regard, he was a thoroughly modern person. Ambiguities and doubts were constant but served to keep him creative. In his later years, Merton intensified his search, suffered a number of tension-induced ailments, and fell passionately in love with a young nurse. Some of these experiences are recapitulated in scene five of *Winter Rain*.

Merton died of accidental electrocution while attending a conference in Bangkok, Thailand. He died on December 10, 1968, twenty-seven years to the day of his entrance into the Abbey of Gethsemani. He was buried at Gethsemani on December 17 in a cold, winter rain.

John XXIII (1881–1963)

The man the world knows as Pope John XXIII (1958–1963) was born Angelo Giuseppe Roncalli on November 25, 1881 in Sotto il Monte, a northern Italian village some ten miles from Bergamo. He was the fourth of thirteen children and the first son of Giovanni Battista and Marianna. The relationships between and among these family members is sketched in the first act of *His Name Is John*.

Roncalli entered the seminary and became a friend of Ernesto Buonaiuti, a classmate. Buonaiuti's ideas and intelligence made him a threat to a Church which had become rigid and insecure under Pope Pius X. Eventually, he was excommunicated and died abandoned by a Church he had sought to serve.

Roncalli was born in the same year as Buonaiuti and identified with many of his ideas. Throughout his life, Roncalli remembered Buonaiuti, wrote about him in his journals and prayed for him, regretting the harshness of the judgment made against him. The relationship of Roncalli and Buonaiuti is dealt with in the first act of *His Name Is John*.

Roncalli was ordained a priest in 1904 and celebrated his first Mass on August 11 of that year, in the crypts of St. Peter's Basilica in Rome, close to the place where he is now buried. He became a secretary to Bishop Radini Tedeschi of Bergamo and made him a model for much of his own life.

During World War I, Roncalli served as a priest-sergeant and chaplain. He reviews this experience at the end of the first act.

Although Roncalli was promoted quickly, it was often for reasons other than esteem for his talents. He was an engaging man but sometimes seemed naive and inept and would be advanced as much to get him out of the way as to reward him.

He was not a favorite of the Mussolini government at a time when the Vatican policy was one of reconciliation. This led to his appointment as Apostolic Visitor to Bulgaria.

This post brought with it the title of "archbishop," an office of some significance for a man of forty-three years of age. Roncalli was to be the first papal representative to Bulgaria in five centuries. Nonetheless, the appointment looked more impressive than it was. It was a form of punishment, removing him as an embarrassment from the Church's center of power and influence. He served in that position for a decade, 1925–1935, and learned there to become sensitive to Orthodox Christianity and to the ecumenical movement.

Roncalli was transferred to Constantinople (1935–1944) where he remained for most of World War II. This nine-year assignment led to heroic action on behalf of persecuted Jews and taught him once again of the need of all the Christian churches to be united in the face of the global problems humanity was suffering in the twentieth century.

The Bulgarian and Turkish experience of Roncalli is recapitulated in the second act of *His Name Is John.*

In the next few years, Roncalli was made nuncio or papal representative to France (1944–1953), patriarch of Venice (1953–1958) and cardinal (1953).

The election of Giuseppe Roncalli to the papacy in 1958, following the death of Pope Pius XII, startled the world. He was a quiet man, approaching eighty, not given to self-promotion, someone who had not said or done very much the world would have deemed impressive.

The first indication that there might be something innovative about his tenure was his choice of a name which had not been used by Popes for centuries. The election speech of John XXIII to his fellow cardinals forms the whole of the third act.

John moved quickly to implement a program of massive

renewal and reform. He frequently acted with unerring instinct and spontaneity rather than from a preconceived plan.

John called for an ecumenical council, the first in a century, and opened its first session in October 1962. He made contact with the communist world and called for the reunion of all Christian churches. He set in motion a revision of church law, issued an encyclical letter on a new economic order for the world (*Mater et Magistra*) and published, weeks before his death, one of the century's most moving statements on world harmony (*Pacem in Terris*).

He was Pope less than five years, one of the shortest pontificates in two millennia of Christian history. Yet he changed the world and the Church profoundly, substantively and irreversibly.

The fourth act of *His Name Is John* concerns itself with these issues.

The death of John on June 3, 1963, at eighty-one years of age, caused sadness in the world, a grief which was not ceremonial only but authentic and personal, a sense of loss experienced by those who never imagined they would mourn the passing of a Pope.

Martin Luther (1483–1546)

The range of Martin Luther's accomplishments is simply astonishing. For all practical purposes, he created the modern German language with his single-handed translation of the New Testament. He composed music of strength and durability and is forever associated with "A Mighty Fortress." He gave the reform movement a simple Mass in the language of the people. He created the first catechism for children and influenced the faith of millions over the centuries by it. He poured into the Christian community and into Western Europe such a torrent of ideas and energy that, five centuries later, they continue to challenge us.

Luther was born on November 10, 1483 in Eisleben, Germany, the son of Hans, a miner and middle-class merchant, and Margaretta, an earnest and pious woman. Luther began to study law at Erfurt but entered a monastery after a religious experience during a terrifying lightning storm in the summer of 1505 (July 2). He was ordained in 1507 and celebrated his first Mass on May 2. The first act of *Summer Lightning* takes place on that day and reviews the early events in the life of Luther and the enduring impact they had on him.

Luther was an Augustinian monk whose superiors recognized and promoted his talent. He became a doctor of theology at a remarkably young age and taught scripture as a professor at the University of Wittenberg.

The dramatic quality of Luther's life was intensified not only by his eloquence but, more, by his tendency to endow theological problems with the passion and complexity of his own life. As his personal struggle and his academic research continued, he found that his central concern was not so much his standing with the Church as his relationship with God. He came to realize (especially in 1508 and 1509) that God's love and mercy are not merited but freely given.

This conviction of Luther about the gratuity of God's goodness caused him to disagree violently with the doctrine of indulgences and the practice of selling them. On October 31, 1517, Luther made public his "Ninety-Five Theses," a wide-ranging challenge to the way the Church was presenting the message of Christ. Luther was startled and gratified by the vehemence and massiveness of the support he received throughout all of Europe, from the very beginning of the protest.

About a year after the "Ninety-Five Theses," Luther had a three-day series of talks with Cardinal Cajetan as Rome began to take notice of the turbulence. This interview was a decisive one and is dealt with in the second act of *Summer Lightning*.

Luther expanded his protest and began in 1519 to deny the supremacy of the Pope and the essential reliability of ecumenical councils. In 1520, Pope Leo X issued the papal bull *Exsurge, Domine* which began the process of Luther's excommunication.

Luther burned the bull in public (December 10, 1520), an action which frames the content of the second act of *Summer Lightning*. There was now no turning back. Excommunication followed in 1521 and Luther was summoned to a major meeting at Worms with the Holy Roman Emperor, Charles V. He uttered there his famous words about his conscience being captive to the word of God.

Luther's complexity can be seen in his wearing of a monk's habit years after his excommunication, even as he developed a program for reform that Rome would find so radical it would allow the Church to split over it. The points of this reform (mainly from his three books: *To The German Nobility; The Babylonian Captivity; The Freedom of the Christian*) are reviewed in the second act of *Summer Lightning*.

Luther married Katherine von Bora on June 27, 1525; he

was almost forty years of age; she was twenty six. They had six children: Hans (1526), Elizabeth (1527), Magdalena (1529), Martin (1531), Paul (1533) and Margaretha (1534). Domestic life brought balance to Luther's sense of himself. The third act of *Summer Lightning* deals with Luther's family life and with his ambivalence about the crushing of the Peasants' Revolt in May and June of 1525.

In spite of the unrelenting intensity of Luther's protest, he was surprised and disappointed that he had, in effect, created a new Church. He had seen himself as a reformer of a Church he loved rather than as an initiator of a wholly autonomous Church structure.

Luther died at Eisleben, the town of his birth, on February 18, 1546. He was sixty-two years of age. The fourth act deals with the death of Luther. Luther died twenty-nine years after he began the Reformation, during the first session of the Council of Trent, Rome's response to Luther.

Because of Luther, Christian history has been substantially altered. Indeed, the history of Europe and of North and South America has been changed by the power and consequences of his thinking.

Many Catholic scholars see Vatican II as Rome's acceptance of Luther's basic reforms but without the fully participatory lay involvement he wanted.

Introduction

There are many ways to deal with Ecclesiology or with a theology of the spiritual life. Philosophy and sociology, psychology and history have at different times played their part in providing a framework for reflections on Church or Christian life.

The oldest approach may still be the best. This is the approach used in the New Testament. It organizes its teaching and themes around personalities. Jesus is, of course, the focal point of a dramatic life story.

The early Christian community might have collected the sayings and parables of Jesus, without organizing them into a biography, and offered these to believers as points to ponder. Much of theology is done this way today: points to ponder, ideas to explore, reasoning processes to follow. There is virtue in this but, one must admit, it appeals to a limited audience and has a limited range.

If one grants this initial observation about the cogency of biography as a vehicle for theology, a second insight might be worth exploring. Theater may be the most direct way of engaging the attention, emotions and minds of people.

The origins of the theater are tied up with religious life and even liturgical celebration. Perhaps this is because an encounter with the human person on such a total, public, deep and communal level may be sensed as holy in its own right.

Theater, furthermore, has a ritual character to it and invites significant participation in other lives, both by actors who submerge themselves in the roles they play and by the audience which vicariously joins the transference. There are creative and perilous exchanges which occur as theater works its magic. Perhaps a better word than "magic" is "mystery."

Theology, in our day, is expressed almost exclusively in academic and scientific categories. Referenced research and methodological procedures are frequently considered at least as important as content. Insights achieved with alternative methods are considered unscholarly or unacademic. Such approaches are dismissed as "popularizing" theology. The implication is that an appeal to people diminishes the worth of the theological enterprise.

Academic theology, of course, has its place and serves well the theological community and even the Church at large. It is the exclusive reliance on this method which may prove detrimental. One need only consider how ill received poetry or drama, fiction or music would be at a professional theological meeting to realize how much resistance many theologians mount against artistic and imaginative life.

Indeed, one might go further and observe that even graceful writing is suspect in most theological circles. Metaphor and symbol, ambiguity and eloquence, passion and inference are avoided.

I have no desire to press the point too sharply. If one can agree that there is at least an element of truth in these remarks, then they have achieved their purpose.

The reader will find in this book the texts of three plays. Work on these plays has been a labor of love. All three plays have been produced professionally on video cassette by Paulist Press with skilled, spirited actors. They have been performed in many different settings and by other actors around the country.

The plays are one-person plays and, therefore, make enormous demands on the actor. On the other hand, it allows the actor a depth of character exploration and a relationship with the audience which are unique.

Until this trilogy of plays, my writing has been confined to prose and to conventional, theological essay form. The process of experiencing how one's text is reinterpreted in drama is startling. A book of theology comes off the press as the author had intended from the time a manuscript was submitted. The author is in control.

Drama, however, is an organic experience. And so the text, even though words are not changed, is modified by staging and filming, by costume and lighting, by direction and musical accompaniment, most tellingly by the actor's interpretation of the lines.

The original text of each play is presented here so that this material will be more widely accessible. It is also offered in this format to assist those people who have written to me after performances and asked that the text be available so that they might read the lines more slowly for whatever benefit that might bring them.

The three figures I have chosen to work with, in these plays, are, in chronological order:

Martin Luther (*Summer Lightning*)
Pope John XXIII (*His Name Is John*)
Thomas Merton (*Winter Rain*)

The plays were produced in reverse order.

I chose these three lives to explore because I believe that the key issues concerning the Church and contemporary spirituality are dealt with by them. I believe also that there is a dramatic quality to these lives, a charm and fascination, that makes them unforgettable. These are people whose lives become their message, whose biography is their theology, whose life is their thought.

The three personalities surveyed in this trilogy of plays are shaped and formed not only by the inner dynamic which drives them but by their relationship with God and the Church. Indeed, it is not only the Church defined in general terms but the Roman Catholic Church specifically which engages their attention and energy.

John XXIII observes, in *His Name Is John*, that nothing can absorb a person more compellingly than the Church of Rome. These three pivotal lives affirm a relationship to that Church. No one of them, although all are reformers, wanted a separate Church. They move across the spectrum from John who gives us visions for the Church rather than dissent, to Thomas Merton who registers dissent and yet obediently submits, to Luther who calls for a reform so radical that a split becomes inevitable. Across this spectrum, there are similarities since all three men are visionaries and dissenters in their own way.

In the turbulence of the present moment, the future belongs to the visionaries and dissenters rather than to those who choose only to manage the Church or to take it back, impossibly, to some supposedly better moment in the past. These three men have this in common: they did not look to the past or even to the present except in terms of the future. They find a pioneer path for God's pilgrim people. In doing this they preserve us from the futility of preferring only the roads which lead back.

The fact that these men continue to speak to so many people, across all Church and religious boundaries, is an indication that they succeeded in what they had to do. The attention that people of good will give them is a sign that people want the Church to be more than a guardian of the past or a preserver of the present. Jesus was neither of these primarily. Nor is the Church in its best tradition.

All three men would have been astonished, in their younger years, if they were told they were destined to be reformers. Luther was a sensitive and pious monk who prayed ardently and kept the rule scrupulously. John XXIII was a devout, almost religiously sentimental Catholic who tended to do what he was told and who served in ministries defined by others. Thomas Merton became a Trappist in a conventional, conservative, effectively cloistered community.

Such lives seemed destined to be lived out in customary, predictable patterns. The fact that they developed as they did is witness to the malleability of the human personality. If grace builds on nature, then nature itself as well as grace can astonish. Where the human and the divine intersect intensively, creativity reaches immeasurable heights.

In essence, the Church is a perilous encounter. It engenders in people longings and visions not readily satisfied by the world at large or the Church in particular. It, therefore, stimulates dissent by its very presence even though this is not consciously its intent. Is it any wonder then that such a Church could produce Luther and John and Merton?

The Church, by its nature, invites people into its community but gives them frames of reference by which the Church is to be affirmed or accused, celebrated or reformed, challenged or obeyed. These frames of reference include God, the Gospel and conscience.

The Church in its tradition makes clear that it is called back to God by its saints, to the Gospel by reformers and to the claims of conscience by prophets. The Church, in its institutional leadership, develops an uneasy relationship with saints, reformers and prophets but does not dismiss them entirely from its life, partly because it cannot, partly because its very institutional leaders are, at times, saints, reformers or prophets. At the risk of categorizing something as complex as a human life too easily, we might see in John XXIII a saint, in Luther a reformer, in Merton a prophet.

As the three men redefine their relationship with the Church they help us redefine ours.

The essence of Luther's reform is the priesthood of all believers, a reform which seeks to give the Church back to the people, a reform which invites the collectivity of the Church to become a true community. For him, the blueprint for this is the Gospel.

The essence of John's vision for the Church is a need to give the Church back to God, to make the Church a pilgrim people longing for God, vaguely discontent with all institutional structures. John loved the notion of the Church as a communion of saints. He asked the Second Vatican Council to include in its document on the Church a chapter on holiness and on the final days and ultimate destiny of the world and the earthly Church. The first decision John made as the Council opened was to insert into the Eucharistic Prayer the name of Joseph, a saint the Church celebrates as its protector. Joseph is to lead the Church home to heaven as once he led the Christ Child safely from Egypt to Nazareth.

The essence of Merton's contribution was a full-hearted response to the claims of conscience. Of the three men, Merton was the most radical in social justice and the most insistent on linking Christianity with other religious and with secular life. Merton's conscience drove him to offer people not only the conjectures of a guilty bystander but the seeds of contemplation sown in the depths of his anguish.

As these men weave the tapestry of their lives, they encounter the Church in terms of their temperaments and training. For Luther, anger and mysticism, rebellion and piety, protest and poetry blend together. In John, quiet diplomacy and subtle suggestion, compassion and compromise, gentleness and resiliency are evident. Merton is intense with conflicting loyalties which lead him from allegiance to the monastery to prayers with Buddhists, from obedience to his abbot to resistance against all institutional oppression.

Luther is all confrontation; John seeks consensus; Merton attempts a contemplative challenge to the world and the Church. The wonderful thing about these three men is the creative manner in which they extend the boundaries of the Church. By going beyond the Church of their own time, they bring the Church beyond itself.

The three men in question envision not only the Church but God with differing perspectives. For Luther, God is an awesome, sovereign even though gracious deity. God offers mercy, it is true, but remains a judge who is not easily satisfied.

For John, God is all love and gentleness, understanding, compassionate and forgiving.

For Merton, God is in the middle of these two attitudes. God can be so demanding that Merton will enter a severe monastery to handle his guilt, settle his internal chaos and justify himself before God. But God becomes, much later, a God who loves all human beings with little reference to their moral misbehavior.

God is, of course, all the divergent values these men designate. And so, through them, we discover again the inadequacy of defining God narrowly.

These perspectives on God are paralleled by corresponding images on the world. Luther, who finds God aloof, creates a theology of the Church which distances it from the world. John envisions an harmonious relationship between Church and state and inspires the Second Vatican Council to produce the most positive statement on the world the Church has ever issued. John found grace in the structures of the contemporary world. Merton fears the world as evil and, in the beginning, censures it and abandons it. Later, as his image of God mellows, he celebrates the world as worthy of affirmation, love and devotion.

As each man faces death, he does so in character. In death, Luther feels lost and asks God to rescue him. He wonders about the rightness of it all and the worthiness of his own life.

John dies as he pleads not for himself, but for a broken Christian world. He affirms love and wholeness in his final words. Merton goes back to his childhood as he dies and asks for connectedness. There is turbulence in his last moments and then a prayer for peace as the restlessness of his life terminates in tranquillity.

The intent of this collection is assistance to university and college audiences but also to religious education and adult discussion groups. It has been my experience that people are more ready for discussion and involvement after a play or movie than they are after they have read a book or listened to a lecture. Drama is less passive.

Allow me to return to the thought which began this essay. The oldest approach may be the most contemporary. In the three figures we meet in this book, we encounter not only their lives but also our own. As we come to terms with Luther, John and Merton we deal with our own humanity and our own call to grace and destiny. To struggle with the same issues as they did is to suffer pain with them but also to achieve liberation and peace. All three plays conclude on a tranquil note. Is there anything more we could ask for the Church and for each of our lives?

Winter Rain

Act One: Harbor
       Set: Railroad Station
Costume: Suit
     Time: December 1941

Pearl Harbor. Such a beautiful name. Good for a poem. Pearl Harbor. Such devastation! War is a horrible business. War again, in my lifetime. Seems so long already. And now the journey to Gethsemane.

The whole world is in its own Gethsemane with the agony of another war, with the blood and sweat of death, with the cold feeling that disaster is near, unavoidable—the end is imminent and the only choice you've got is how you accept it.

My journey to Gethsemane is different. Gethsemane for me is not a garden but an abbey, not agony but healing, not anguish but home, paradise, a Pearl Harbor, safe, peaceful— the pearl of great price, the harbor of tranquillity. I want that for the whole world. Is it wrong to have this for myself, when the whole world is without joy?

Not much joy in this train station. Such a cold December night! All the symbols of loneliness crowd me: alone, darkness, freezing rain, trains.

I like the way Thomas Wolfe writes of trains: metaphors of the solitary human journey, a hurried flight across the landscape of the earth, a whistle wailing in the fearful blackness, a flutter of lights and then emptiness and echoes. Trains are haunting engines of loss and absence.

So much poetry in me tonight. Guess I'm excited. That makes words tumble along.

Would she be surprised! Why do I think of her now when I'm further than ever from everything her world embraced? A war was beginning then also. I don't remember it, of course. We were in France and I was born to two hapless artists. France was not a good place to be during the Great War. That's how Hemingway would say it. Not a good place.

She was right about getting us out of there—that was one time I have to admit she was right. I was only a year old. She carried me out of France. She had to hold me. I was too young to walk. She had to hold me then and carry me out of France, across the Atlantic, through clusters of U-boats and clouds of fear into New York Harbor and destiny. I'd be free of her in New York—for a while.

New York Harbor is a long way from Pearl Harbor. Funny how I keep moving east—from France to New York—now from New York to Kentucky. Or is it west? You have to go west to get to the east. At least I do.

Pearl Harbor is in the Pacific. Guess I'll never see the Pacific. Kentucky and Gethsemane will be as close as I get.

The train. Finally. My last train ride.

No more travel. No more journeys. I've got to get off the damn road. I'll be in Gethsemane for the rest of my life. The rest of my life. That's what I need. I need rest. Need to stop running.

I'll never see New York again. Good. So much happened here. I have a strange affection for New York, mingled with fear. I grew up in New York, was baptized here, graduated Columbia, began my career as a professor. I learned to be tough here, and tender. I wrote poems and a dissertation. She died here. I wrote novels here and got sick of sex here. It's not a good place anymore. And so I leave it.

And it doesn't even pay me the compliment of noticing my absence.

(*Merton is now on board the train.*)

Is this seat vacant?

Thank you.

Doesn't look like I'll get into much of a conversation with him. Good. No friendly reminders of New York. Not in a mood to talk anyway. Too much going on in my own mind. Monks look better when their mouths are shut. Certainly Trappists do. Funny name for a monastery where you're not allowed to talk. Trappist. Keep your trap shut. Don't get trapped. Trappist. I like their official name better. "Cistercian." That sounds elegant, aloof, mysterious. How the hell am I going to do it, not talking forever? I'm such a good talker. Give me a drink and I'll talk you into anything. That's how they're going to keep me quiet. No liquor. I could use a drink right now. Sitting next to this—fellow. He's the one they ought to shut up for good. No one would miss him.

Who's going to miss me? Maggie? I hope so. Is that wrong?

Am I really going to be a monk? It's crazy. Tom Merton, man of the world. Tom Merton who could drink half the world under the table. And who chased the better half around the globe. All that alcohol and sex won't mix easily with holy water and fasting. I hope it's different this time. I've had too many dreams shattered to be able to handle any more hope. The whole country is having a dream shattered this week. Pearl

Harbor. Death must have been so quick. A lot of people were burned. Maybe that's when death is worst. You expect the next moment to be as ordinary as the last and death walks in and it's all over.

It must be saddest of all to die in December, near Christmas, in the cold. Tough to burn to death. I guess I'm not a spiritual person. Monks are supposed to handle death easily. I'm not sure I will. I know she didn't.

I was only six when she died. She made such a damn mess of it. I mean, for God's sake, she didn't even say goodbye. Wouldn't let me near her. Well, she was always that way. I thought it might have been different if she were dying. But it wasn't. One day my father came home from the hospital. That sad face. I can still see it. He loved her a lot. I guess he was the best thing that ever happened to her—or to me, for that matter. He painted such bright scenes. All sunshine and color. Right through the war. He made me believe in light. Glad I didn't get his name. "Owen" is a lot harder to live with than Thomas. She hated "Thomas." It always had to be "Tom." Even the birth certificate reads "Tom." In the middle of all that French.

Hell, my thoughts are all over the lot.

It's a funny kind of feeling. It's like dying, going to Gethsemane. A death to the world, to the self. A death to hard liquor and soft women. I don't mind that kind of dying. At least tonight I don't.

But I also feel that everything is beginning. I feel new and fresh, eager, happy. I never had a home, never belonged anywhere. I feel like a kid who just got adopted and is about to find a family and home for the first time.

Yes. Of course, I intend to pay. I was so deep in my own thoughts I didn't see you. I've got the ticket somewhere. Just give me a chance to find—maybe you can come back to me in a few minutes—Oh no, wait, here it is. Okay! Okay?

He gave me a letter when he came in the house. My father gave me a letter with a lot of tears and emotion. I was only six—and he gave me a letter. It was the strangest letter I got in my life. The saddest. The worst. The one I wished I never received. Why did she *write?*

Well, I took this letter. My father suggested I read it alone somewhere.

I wish he had his arm around me when I read it. I had never received a letter from mother before. I recognized the handwriting. I did well with reading, but that was usually with books, with printing. It was hard to read, slow, painful. I was confused and frightened. I started to shiver. Could not grasp all of it. My mother was informing me, by mail, that I would never see her again. She was going to die.

This was her goodbye to me.

She was sick. I knew she was sick, very sick. But death is something I somehow never expected. I cried. Became depressed. Such a heavy sorrow. I can feel it now when I think about it. Not only the death. But that she did not care enough to want to see me. That she could not bring herself to touch me at the end, to talk of love and meaning and missing. That she did not let me cry in her arms. I've cried in the arms of more women than I can number since then. It was less about sex than about touching. Less a sign of strength than a need to be cared for.

Uh—oh, coffee? No—yes, I think I will. Black. Thanks.

Maybe all this will come back to haunt me in the monastery. If they let me write, maybe my readers will care for me.

Who wants to read the books of a monk? Damn it! I want to be a writer, a good writer, the best writer monastic life ever produced. I want everyone to know Tom Merton. To prove to her I was better than she thought. To show she was wrong to have demanded so much and given so little.

Hell, I can get petty. I'm still having temper tantrums. Oh mom, why did you write, when you could have held me?

Act Two: Mountain
    Set: Simple Room in the Monastery
Costume: Trappist Habit
    Time: 1948

It hit the top of the charts. My autobiography made it. *Seven Storey Mountain*. The reviews are great. New York Times best seller list. Week after week.

Tom Merton's a great writer. Evelyn Waugh loved it!

Would you believe I've been in the monastery seven years! Monks are not supposed to be so vain. Or so popular. I'm happy all this has happened. But I'm also frightened. Way down deep I know there's something destructive about all this.

The other day some of the younger monks asked me how I would complete the sentence, "I am . . ." Some kind of crazy psychological test. You know what I said? "I am Thomas Merton, the famous writer." There was an embarrassed silence after that! They were confused and I was revealed in a way that was awkward. Didn't think of using my religious name, "Louis." That shocked everyone. I'm still Tom Merton in my own mind—the guy who rang the bell here seven years ago and asked them if they would take me in, the guy who chose to use his own name on his books rather than write anonymously or under a religious name.

"Tom Merton, the famous writer." Imagine! Not Tom Merton, the monk or contemplative. I hate to admit this—and I'd never tell the abbot—but I'd rather be a writer than a monk. I'm committed to the monastery, but it would all die without the writing. I'm a better writer than a monk, because that's what I'd prefer to be.

How do I live with all this? How do I dare make the native talent more important than the chosen way of life? How do I call myself a contemplative when I want books more than I want grace? This terrible need in me to be honest with myself sickens me. I don't like what I see, but I'm forced to look. I won't lie to myself—even for pious reasons. Is that arrogance? Or humility?

So many contradictions. Circles in circles in circles.

O.K. So I'm ill at ease with myself. The problem with a lot of people around here is that they try to keep me from becoming what I'm supposed to be. The abbot does, and most of my readers do. They want a monk who's very— monkish. Monkey business. That's what they want. A per- formance.

Well, I won't perform. It's not the schedule or the routine or the fasting or the celibacy or the prayers that make a good monk. It's what you do with who you are. That's what makes you good—period. I won't be good on schedule or perform in a monastic circus for an audience that looks in on my life but doesn't really know or care about the inner me, the person God has given a vocation to, a vocation to be himself.

That's why my mother didn't like me. She was my first abbot. I wouldn't jump through the hoop. I'm not a seal. I'm a human being. I'm a writer. I'm Tom Merton, the famous writer. And I'm not going to apologize for it! Except to myself. I guess I am rather defensive. But someone has to defend me! Here I am yelling at myself—trying to be certain that I hear what I'm trying to say to others.

I like the attention writing brings me. Okay. But some- thing else is going on. It sounds self-serving when I say it. Maybe it is. It sounds like a justification after the crime. But something else *is* going on. When I write, I touch God—I find the inner me, the true self, the guy who was here before he was a monk—the person behind the mask—the light beyond the shadow—the truth beneath the disguise.

I guess I'm a heretic. But I'm trying to do something for myself and others that needs to be done. I'm trying to say that holiness has something to do with passion. That maybe some of the robots in this monastery are further from God than a lot of people in the world. God can't be that easily manipulated to perform as we want God to perform by whatever monastic schedule or rule we devise. It's what you become passionate about and die for, what you become involved in and suffer for, what you rejoice in with all your being. That's what matters. How you live!

That's why sex was wrong for me. There was no passion or commitment, no suffering or joy. Only anarchy. And I drank to drown the emptiness.

So I write and it purifies my soul. I write and I feel unworthy of what I've written. I write and I sense it's okay for me to be a monk. I write and I live. That's what matters.

Life is too big for a monastery! So many people muffle the music, stifle the song, choke on the words, stammer into silence so that others will accept them. I'm a hermit in my heart, a solitary explorer. I'm not going to live my life by norms from another century. We did a lot of good things in *this* century. I want to live in the present.

So I'm on the lists. The book is selling. And the mail is monumental. It's my life they're reading. And they're reading about someone who cared enough not to be indifferent, about a man who had enough passion to walk a road no one tried before, about a monk who left the secular world because it did not have enough passion, about a contemplative who won't let a monastery kill his emotion or his longing to be himself.

Luther was a monk. Maybe I'm supposed to go the same way.

I'm angry about exploitation of negroes. And no one cares. I'm sick about the last war and the monster we exploded on Hiroshima. I'm sick with all the things that make us secure. One thing you learn as a contemplative. You can count on nothing. You don't control the process. When you do, you're in trouble. Control. That's what's behind the hell of Harlem and the horror of Hiroshima. Control another race with power or prejudice or with a bomb against which there is no defense.

If I let them control me, I become involved in the syndrome of control that makes us sick. If I give in, they begin to think human lives are predictable and human beings ought to conform. One way to keep control out of their hands is to write an autobiography that makes everyone responsible for your life. When everyone's involved in your life, no one controls it. I'm going to become a saint—but in a way that doesn't fit the rules.

So here I am—seven years in the monastery and already a "worldly" monk. If I'm good at what I'm supposed to be, I'll make it as a monk. If I've got to give up what I'm meant to be, it won't matter what kind of monk I was.

Act Three: East
      Set: Living Room with a Cocktail Party
  Costume: Clerical Garb
     Time: 1964

Yes, I would like some more tea. No, the trip was not very difficult. It was not difficult because of the expectation—and the memories. This is my first return to New York since my departure for Gethsemane many years ago—twenty-three years ago, to be exact. I have changed much. But the trip here was a joy. As the plane circled New York City, I kept saying to myself, "I'm home. I'm home." Don't know what that all means. I once left here looking for home and found it in the monastery. Maybe both places are home and I have to get them together before I'm really safe. Getting opposites together. That's what I need now in my life.

You're a Buddhist and I'm a Christian. You're Dr. Suzuki, the famous scholar from the east, and I'm Tom Merton, the writer from the west. I want to know why I find a compatibility between things my church tells me I should find incompatible. Do I find this because I'm arrogant or because I'm spiritual? Because I'm narrow or because I have vision? I feel as though I'm going to confession—to a Buddhist.

I went to Gethsemane to find simplicity and freedom. Now I'm complicated and confined. Part of the reason why I'm here is because I went there. So the road I have taken has not been the wrong one.

Yes, I agree. There are no wrong roads. I once thought there were, that the whole world was a wrong road and most of the people in the world were misdirected.

I see God now as an inner gyroscope in each life—as a compass that directs the human heart safely.

I once thought that God and the spiritual life were for few people. The monastery was an exotic experience, a romantic ideal, a utopian community, an experiment flung in the teeth of a culture that was excluded from it. Contemplation was for heroes and for saints, for celibates and cloistered clerics. For nobody, you see. That's what made it so appealing. I was doing what nobody else was doing. I was special, chosen, unique, different, grand, wild, reckless, free.

(*Merton is offered something to eat.*)

Thank you.

A few years ago I was in Louisville, in Kentucky, a city not far from our monastery. I was in the street with many people and I felt an overwhelming sense of oneness with them. It was the most profound religious experience of my monastic life. And it happened outside the monastery. I shouted to myself: "I'm like them. And they're like me. I don't want to be different. Or better."

I was shaken to the depths by the experience. Somehow it was all wrong. How could I go on being a monk if it made no difference? Then the thought struck me that people don't get married to be different, or enter professions to be different. They do what they do because it has significance in itself, even if it is no different or even better than what everyone else is doing.

My Church does not understand enough about the ordinary for me to learn there what I need to know now. I don't wish to be a Buddhist, but I need to be a man. I need to be assured that the human dimension in all of us is worthy, and that grace is God's gift to those who never suspect they are different. I cannot learn in Buddhism all that I need to know, but, between Christianity and Buddhism, I can learn what I require for the next step in the journey.

I am confused, but I also feel I have been enlightened. My journey goes on. If I turn off the road, I shall be lost. I'm going to be searching till I die. Buddhists don't find that surprising—but we in the West believe monks ought to be settled.

(Merton is offered something to drink.)

Yes. I would like more tea.

I wish you would come to our monastery. That you would speak to our monks. But that is not possible. But one day we shall learn together that God made none of us very different. So divisions and conflicts are never justified. It's not the truth that separates—but blindness and pride and the fear of knowing how much alike we are.

Any chance of getting a rug in here? I'm not asking for luxury. It's only a cinder-block hideaway. With all the money I've brought into the monastery, you'd think they'd buy me a carpet.

Thank you for the chairs, Roger. Did they give you a hard time? I figured as much. Tell them I won't sit when I visit the monastery. That'll make up for the chair I took.

I've wanted this place for longer than I can remember.

If someone told me when I was a student at Columbia that I'd be a hermit some day, I'd think him as weird as a lot of people think I am now. But a lot of these same people dream of getting away alone. A lot of people find aspects of monastic life attractive. Certainly a lot of people would like to have written books or walked out on the whole damn world.

But, see, I'm not going to do it that way. I'm not here to escape but to harass. We're going to start a peace movement from here. This is headquarters for Non-Violence U.S.A. The irony of it all! The Pentagon has made Kentucky an armed camp. The one enemy the military never built a defense system against is hermits. How the hell do you detect a hermit on a radar screen? Even they'd feel uncomfortable attacking a hermitage.

I've got to be careful not to enjoy this too much. But I love changing things. It's even fun moving your own chair around in your own cinder-block palace.

I'd like to change the abbot while I'm busy changing the world.

It's wonderful having a sense of home, of belonging.

There's a terrible urgency in me that drives me to challenge settled systems. I've got the feeling that I don't have much longer to live. I'm fifty now. A milestone. I think of all the roads I've never followed, roads which are lost now, irretrievable—except by my longing for them.

It feels like autumn in my bones, with the chill of death in the air.

I've never found the peace I was looking for—even here in the abbey where I belong. I don't know where else to look. I've come to believe it will elude me till the end.

But, if I could bring peace to others—maybe that's enough. Sometimes you have to be willing to look on from the outside and to be happy that others got what you wanted more desperately than you'd let on. Maybe such an attitude has something to do with Christ or goodness or human decency.

I wouldn't mind dying if it'd stop the Vietnam War. I'd give my life to stop it—as an atonement, a sacrifice. But what is one more life when so many have died already? I wouldn't mind dying if it would help defuse the monster bombs. I wrote a book a few years ago—a long meditation to be scratched on the walls of a cave—a reflection on what it means to live near nuclear disaster.

I wouldn't mind dying even if I myself never experienced a world in which peace was assured. Such an ancient dream. A myth dream. I wouldn't mind dying at all if such a world would come to pass. I've been surrounded by war for fifty years. There was a war on when I was born and when I came into the monastery. And, after that, a war in Korea, and now in Vietnam. My brother was killed in a war.

And so I'm a survivor of the century's nightmare—a bystander the bombs missed—someone who feels guilty since he has no wounds—all the scars are internal.

A whole bunch of pacifists are coming this afternoon. We're beginning a peace movement—and I can't get enough chairs! Dorothy Day's excited by the prospect of a Catholic peace movement. Somehow I'm become the guru of the group, the Gandhi of Gethsemane. Hermits against H-bombs! That'd confuse them. We're going to organize and to make life uncomfortable for all those who want to exterminate it.

Would you believe there are a lot of Catholics out there, some of them with hierarchical household names, who are frightened about what I'm doing?

Imagine becoming anxious about hermits! Being scared of people struggling for non-violence. Bishops for the Bomb! What a travesty! When Christ took the sword out of Peter's hand, he disarmed every Christian soldier. Christ didn't come to let the killing go on. The same guys who demand capital punishment for the crime of homicide applaud as virtuous those who slaughter thousands.

They tell me I'm too political. If I said my prayers well, they suppose they'd never hear from me. They'd like that. Irony! Irony! Irony! How do you shut up a monk who has a vow of perpetual silence? How do you tell a hermit to be quiet?

Gandhi said you can't be holy in the twentieth century unless you helped change the political order. Christ took on the politics of Jerusalem and Rome. They wanted him to say his prayers, too. But he said short ones and was back again in the marketplace. When you don't cause trouble in a world as troubled as today's world, you're in trouble.

How can I sit still here and meditate when six million innocent Jews were exterminated? How can I be silent when my fellow countrymen nuclear bombed Japanese cities? How can I act as though I knew nothing when I've seen with my own eyes the hell hole we made in Harlem? I love this nation too much to praise it when it destroys lives. I believe in "liberty and justice for all" too ardently to put an American stamp of approval on atrocity and genocide. I'm going to shout until I embarrass them and shame them and paralyze them with guilt. I'm going to yell loud enough to split atom bombs to pieces!

I'm not going to let a cardinal silence me when the Gospel of Christ is on fire in me. If I'm a zealot or a nut—if I'm a fanatic or a lunatic—so be it! But I'm going to be what I have to be. If God made me nutty, then I'm going to be the best damned nut this monastery has ever seen.

More people died in wars in this century than in all the previous wars put together. In fifty years of my lifetime, we killed with a savagery that history had not witnessed before. Well, it's got to stop. We've got to stop calling it virtue. Maybe the world needs a nut to recognize the lunacy of it all. We've killed till our arms ached. We killed so many we didn't have tears for them all, and we ran out of names—so we killed by numbers. We killed so many children and parents, we made the world an orphan.—And now we're getting ready for a bigger war, with better bombs.—We can kill millions in minutes.

God, give me the words, the voice, the steady hand, the courageous heart to do something. For the sake of all who died. For the sake of all about to die. Make me die instead of them. God, more than anything else in the world, I want peace—if not for me, at least for them.

Act Five: Love
    Set: Hermitage, Typewriter on the Table
Costume: Trappist Habit
    Time: 1967

Dear Father Abbot: With this letter, I wish to begin the process of my resignation from the monastery. Perhaps you are as surprised as I am by this turn of events. I know you will be relieved. We have not been the best of friends and, I am sure, I have not become the monk I might have been. What may surprise you more is that I am grateful for you. There is chaos in me, an anarchy that needed a strong hand to control. I can't be sure your motives were noble, but the end result helped me. You were often unreasonable. But so am I. I believe at times you were petty. But so am I. We may have provoked each other to do things we might otherwise have avoided.

There are, of course, others to think of besides ourselves. There are other monks. You told me the other day that they consider me a faithful monk and are often inspired by what I do. I thank you for telling me. I treasure these words more than I can say. They are in my heart till the end. But these words also create an obligation. I shall disappoint them. Especially the younger monks I trained. But, if they heard me well, they will realize that I did not train them to be *my* disciples.

I worry about my readers and those I have guided. They must know somehow that all I have written has been the truth as I know it. They must see what I do now as another form of the truth. There have been sixty books over the last twenty years. I have been obsessed with writing. But, without the writing, I would never have stayed as long—or grown, I believe, so much. Without the writing we might have been better friends. The loss of that friendship may well be the cost we have paid for what each of us knew to be right.

And, of course, there is Margaret. I love her, but I do not resign because of her. Nor shall I marry her. I think I have lost along the way the capacity to be self-giving. I have lived so long with my books and my silence and my own projects that I have no space left to bring in someone else permanently. There is a great sadness in me because of this. But it is, perhaps, better this way. If others knew of her, it would make their understanding of what I am doing too easy. It is not easy. But I believe it is right.

My life has been a series of conflicting loyalties. And she came in the middle of my commitments with her demands that I be more human. She brought me peace—but it will not last. And I could not give her tranquillity.

I believe she represents a part of me that died when my mother sent me that devastating letter. I needed a woman to hold me the way she never did. But I am more like my mother than I would like to think. I would demand too much and give too little. Maybe God has become important for me in a way that excludes significant commitments to people. This is sad. And it may not be right. But I believe it has happened.

I cry for her at night—but I will not go to her at night.

And so the issue is settled. And Margaret shall cry about it as I have wept about it. But the tears are more merciful than marriage would be. The pain of today will pass away more easily than years of disappointment.

I have written to her about all of this. But I feel I owe you an explanation as well.

You will feel, no doubt, as this letter goes on, that you are being asked to read, not a letter, but another book. Be patient with me. I am a writer, and I do that better than I speak. Besides, if we were together we would become angry with each other, or I might become reticent because you are not an easy man to be around when I feel vulnerable.

I know you were harassed by other abbots and by Rome, by cardinals and bishops, by letters from angry Catholics—and all of this because of my writing or social protests, my visits with folk singers and civil rights leaders, my letter to Boris Pasternak, and my defense of optional celibacy, my resistance against the Vietnam War and my anger at the arms race and my acceptance of Oriental religions.

And so it is better that I end the experiment, that I no longer burden the community with this hapless hermit who could not keep his mouth shut.

I need to get away from everything and everyone. To wander in the desert or become anonymous in the city. I need to give everything up again. But this time I'm not as sure as I was before that it will be worth the sacrifice. I need to light a fire and burn the past in a holocaust of flame without knowing whether the end result will be glory—or ashes.

My faith is no longer a string of certitudes. It is a series of doubts which somehow never become denial. I know God is there ambiguously *and* assuredly. I have become capable of understanding my contemporaries who believe and make promises, who live life and define fidelity tentatively. Faith may be no less real for us because we hesitate and attach conditions, reconsider and question the whole process. We may be less sure because we are more personal, less institutional about it all, because we offer vulnerability rather than invincibility. Faith is a way of being, and the way we were in this century is qualified. We see faith as less a predictable pattern than people once supposed it was.

In any case, I'm not settled. But you may be more settled, now that you're rid of me. I have been told I'm a clever person.

This may be so—but I am not a wise one. There is something reckless, almost self-destructive, in me, something that makes me do things with all my heart rather than moderately or reasonably. And all my heart went into this monastery. I shall not get it back. My life cannot be unbound from this monastery. And should not be.

And so I set forth. With regrets, undeniably. With songs of gratitude for what was, and, I confess, a measure of relief. With more memories than hopes, with fewer friends than I once had—and with no clear vision.

I shall sign this letter, "Father Louis." It was a name I used on none of my books. But it was the name my brothers in the monastery used when they wanted me to know that they and I were one. It is a name that belongs here. It is Father Louis I leave behind, but Thomas Merton who goes forth. I shall miss Louis. More than you do. I leave him here in the hope that he might help you think kindly now and again of Tom Merton and, when you do, that you might pray for him. Respectfully.

~~Father Louis. . . .~~

Thomas Merton

(Merton realizes the error in the signature and laughs at the foolishness and at the revelation involved in the error.)

Act Six: Home
  Set: Chapel with Trappist lying on a board which serves as a casket
Costume: blue jeans and work shirt
  Time: 1968

And so I shall die a monk after all. An answer to the great question.

I can feel life ebb from me. And I am all alone once again. It is fitting that it end this way. But I wish it were different. Closer to Pearl Harbor than Gethsemane. I'm in the Pacific somewhere. Where? The East. The perilous East. The perilous pearl. The pearl of great price.

I die like a criminal. Electrocuted. Christ died like a criminal. My flesh burned as shock after shock hit me. Nails into hands and feet. Shock after shock. Like hammers against my body. I could smell the burning of my own body. It must have been the fan, the loose wire, bad connections. Bad connections all my life.

O God. I'm so far from home. I never found the pearl harbor—harbor home—harbor—me. Mother, why didn't you hug me? I miss Gethsemane—the agony—the grace. Dad? I'm dying. Abba—father—

Ring the bell. Let me in. For whom it tolls. Let me in. Take me home, Father. Father Abbot, I want to be a monk. Bring me peace.

Will no train ever come to this station? No train to take me home. No trains to Pearl Harbor. Mama, why didn't you hug me?

Dad? O Dad, paint me a picture. Let me see the sunshine. Once more. A ray of light. Don't leave me alone.

Bring me into one of your pictures. Peaceful pictures. Pictures—so bright.

I'm glad I never sent the letter. What did I do with it? I'm glad I die a monk. An answer to the great question.

O God, take the pain and bring peace to the world. Help the pain help me—to forgive my mother and the monastery and all those who hurt me as they did good. Make the pain mean something more than this cold I feel and the darkness that makes me despair.

Was I proud to have written so well of me and so poorly of others? Was I immature to have valued my life and disregarded others? Conflicting loyalties. There was too much to be loyal to, too many fidelities, too many commitments, too many loves, too many needs, too much of me. Not enough. I never did enough. I wrote sixty books and never found the right words. Traveled all the way to Asia, here in Thailand, and didn't see enough. Never enough. I ran out of life before the loyalties were satisfied. I ran so fast the road left me—still running when the road ran out and there was nowhere to go. There were other things to do and I had no more time. No more time. The final minutes.

Conflicting loyalties. What do I remain faithful to for the last few minutes? I kept the celibacy. But I'm not sure it was a victory.

I stayed a monk. But I don't know if it was right. I only know it happened. I can't fathom it out. Especially now. Where am I anyway? Dad, one of your bright pictures. We need a bright picture. It's getting dark and no one is lighting any more lights. Dad, bring me a bright picture. Take me with you this time when you go far away to paint your pictures. Pain. Paint. So much pain when you go away to paint. Mama, put down the pen. Don't write. Not right for you to write. Wrong writing. Pain writing. Don't write. Hold me. I'm so cold. Don't you be cold to me.

O God, I loved you. Through all the crazy, turbulent, impossible events, I loved you. You were the thread that held it all together. You held me when others would not hold me. I sought you at dawn and pursued you in the daylight and prayed to you in the darkness. Walk with me, on this final road, on the last bend.

I don't know if I did what was right but I know I wanted to. And now you are the only one that is left. The loneliness would have been so much worse if you had not stayed nearby.

Maybe I was a good monk after all. I truly believe I never lost you. I followed you through the West into the East. From Europe to America, to Asia. From the confusion of my early years to the complexities of my later life. You went into purgatory with me and guided me through the Seven Storey Mountain and kept me company in Gethsemane. You were with me at the train stations of life and you made me dream of paradise and a pearl harbor. You were the goal I grasped and lost, but never stopped reaching for.

And now the journey is done. The train comes to a halt. This is the harbor we anchor in, near the shore of safety. It is so quiet.
I trusted you everytime I was lost. And I feel so lost now. Ring the bell. Take me home.
I'm cold and frightened. Not of you, but of my own inadequacy. I have no—adequacy—left.

O God, put Father Louis and Thomas Merton together and take me home. Beyond Gethsemane—to peace.

Discussion Questions

- The opening scene portrays a restless, agitated young man on his way to spend the rest of his life "in silence" in a monastery. Did you find his uncertainty uncomfortable? In your opinion, is an atmosphere of disquietude and questioning conducive to making a vocational choice? Explain your answer.

- The play refers to Merton's rejection by his mother (whether real or imagined), suggesting this as an influence and motivating factor in his search for intimacy with God. In your opinion, what effect can such a situation have on a person's journey of faith?

- There appears to be a correlation made between Merton's journey of faith and his journey to Gethsemane. What do trains evoke for Merton? What evocative forces are you aware of in your life?

- "The whole world is in its own Gethsemane." In your opinion, is Merton's concern for the world incongruous with his decision to enter a Trappist monastery? Explain your answer.

- In Act 2 we see Merton seven years after entering Gethsemane. What changes, if any, have you noticed? Are the concerns Merton expressed in Act 1 still his concerns in Act 2? Have new concerns emerged? Is Merton free of his past? What concern lingers from your past?

- Review what you have learned about Merton's early life and his reasons for choosing a monastic vocation. What does the play suggest about the significance of Merton's writings for him? How do you express your "inner self"?

- Merton struggled with control in regard to his life. Recall some of the people who were part of Merton's inner conflict. Comment on this in reference to the statement, "God is an inner gyroscope . . . that guides the human heart safely."

• In Act 3 Merton is back home in New York City and still does not feel safe. What are some of the indications of this? When do you feel "safe"?

• Merton's Louisville experience as expressed in this image was significant for him. In your view, what effect did it have on Merton?

• Merton states, "I'll be searching until I die." For what is he searching at this point in his life? What are you searching for?

• Is there any observable change in Merton from Act 3 to Act 4?

• Merton saw solitude as a means to closeness with others as well as God. Comment on this.

• At the end of Act 4 Merton's prayer demonstrates the depth of his caring for others. What were some of the events in his life that you think contributed to his strong sense of solidarity with those who suffer?

• Jesus offered his life in atonement for us. Merton also wants to sacrifice himself for others. He says, "I wouldn't mind dying for others." Are there any other parallels you can make between Jesus and Merton after reading this play cassette? Do you ever feel this way?

• What did Act 5 contribute to your understanding of monastic life? Did anything surprise you? In what manner was your vision of a monk's life widened?

- What are your feelings now in regard to Merton's spiritual journey? What does the information contained in Acts 5 and 6 contribute to your understanding of how one grows in intimacy with God?

- Is the Merton seen in death the same Merton we saw in life? Explain your position.

- The events of Merton's life flow rapidly through his mind after death. What do you think about his experiencing of suffering, doubt, and fear after his death, his wrenching away from self toward complete trust in God? What teaching of the Catholic Church does this suggest to you?

- Merton prays, "Put Fr. Louis and Thomas Merton together and take me home." What is your reaction to this?

- Discuss the five stages of the mystical life—(1) awakening, (2) purgation, (3) illumination, (4) dark night, and (5) union—in relationship to Merton's journey of faith, and especially in regard to any correlation they might have to this final image of Merton after death.

His Name Is John

Act 1: *Origins*
Set: *Vatican Office of the Pope*
Costume: *White Cassock*
Time: *1963*

One of my earliest memories—my father hoisted me on his shoulders to see a parade. It was one of my best memories of him.

We were not close. I was the eldest son, the first boy, the fourth of twelve children.

My father was a hard worker.

I looked often for another father—not to supplant mine, only to supplement a little.

He must have cared more than I realized. Would a father hold his son on his shoulders if he did not care?

Sometimes I feel that as Pope I would like to hold the world on my shoulders. But then that would make me too important.

Perhaps, a child on my shoulders. Or someone small and frightened in a world that bewilders all of us.

How many people in my life held me on their shoulders? But then I grew too heavy and they found it easier to put an arm around me.

I was born in 1881, ten miles from Bergamo, in northern Italy—a little town I took with me wherever I went, Sotto il Monte. It means "at the foot of the mountain" in Italian. I climbed to higher places when my father's shoulders were not available.

We have to climb on shoulders and mountains when we

know we're not big enough for the world. Jesus looked kindly on Zacchaeus who had to climb a sycamore tree to catch a glimpse of the Lord.

I was born on November 25 at 10:15 in the morning. They called me "Angel Joseph"—Angelo Giuseppe. The world knows me by another name.

A lot of troublemakers were born in 1881. Teilhard de Chardin, the French Jesuit priest theologian, was silenced by the Church. I rather liked his work but most people here at the Vatican did not. He was too optimistic, they said. Not enough about sin. They say the same thing about me. Naive. Trusts people too much. But they can't silence a Pope. How would that look? I can't be silenced—one of the benefits of the job. There are those who think I should be silenced, not because of my theology, just out of mercy to others. I talk too much.

Chardin said the modern age was valuable and that the world would find its way—directed by an energy that made all of us more aware and loving. There is evil, of course. But evil has a less sturdy hold on people than goodness.

And so I like Chardin but I try to be discreet. I keep feeling I'll disappoint the Pope if he hears about this. And then I recall who the Pope is and I smile.

As a student, I was a good friend of Ernesto Buonaiuti. He was also born in 1881 but he had a worse time of it than Chardin. They, we excommunicated him.

(Flashback: Seminary Garden)

Ernesto, you and I were young men at a bad time in the Church. The new century had just begun. And the Church was insecure. Science made us look and feel absurd. It seemed as though there was no need for God anymore. In order to defend our faith, we isolated ourselves from the intellectual world. We spread suspicion not only about thinkers but about the very adequacy of the human mind itself.

I remember the time when the seminary faculty ripped out the pages of a book you were reading in the history of philosophy! They didn't want you to read about Peter Abelard and his love for Heloise. Abelard shook the twelfth century theological world with his willingness to hear the heretics.

In the Council I called as Pope, I remembered you, Ernesto. I invited those we once called "heretics" and asked for their assistance. I needed Protestants and Jews to help me become a good Pope. You would have liked that.

They were bad times, Ernesto. You were too honest for them. In bad times, even the good learn to dissemble; it is not the evil nor even the good who are vulnerable; it is the innocent who are most often destroyed.

They were bad years and they lasted too long. So long that few of us who lived through them could be called entirely blameless.

Ernesto, in this you were right. In this, I, the Pope, learned from you. No more inquisitions. Never again. No more crusades. No more cruelty for Christ's sake. In the name of God, no more pain.

This cancer wastes my body and I think of you tonight and write about you in my journal.

Ernesto, you stood by my side when I was ordained a priest. You were my official assistant. And yet you were unfrocked, dismissed, excommunicated, censured and condemned. You died when I was Papal Nuncio to France. They told me you asked the windows to be opened so you might die hearing the Easter bells.

You heard the bells but no one spoke to you of love and mercy. Don Ernesto, Father Ernesto, my friend and my brother priest—you died without cross or candles, no priest to bless your body, no ceremony from the Church for your funeral. Even in death, we were not capable of compassion. Why did you frighten us so much?

(Return to 1963 and Vatican Office)
And so I keep my journal. I write of all this sixty-two years after we first met. What does all this say about us, about me, about this Church?

1881. I was born that year—and Chardin—and Ernesto.

My mother's name was Marianna. I loved her, of course. But you must understand: there is no organization in the world which so absorbs a man as the Church of Rome. And so I did a good deal of my growing up without her. But you must know how much she meant to me. A grown man can call for his mother when he is in trouble the way he did as a child.

I called her name when I was elected Pope.

(Flashback: Turn-of-the-Century Kitchen)
The earliest memory I have was her bringing me to a shrine when I was four years old. "Look", she said, "Angelino, little Angel, look how beautiful the Madonna is." She took all of us: Teresa was six, Ancilla five, my younger brother Zaverio two, Maria Elisa one. Mama was pregnant with another child. She lifted me so I could see. Mothers do that so well. "Look, Angelino, look, little angel. See. See. Guarda. Guarda."

I thought of her too at my coronation—when they lifted me in the *sedia*, the huge chair. Now it was not mama who lifted me for the Madonna or father for the parade but the

Church for its own life. It was not Angelino the little boy, but an old man named John, newly named—John XXIII. Lift him high. Hold him steady. Viva il Papa. Viva il Papa. Viva. Viva.

I was nineteen when she gave me the sternest tongue-lashing of my life. She said I no longer cared for her, that I disliked her, that I showed no gentleness. I gave her further reason for this when, soon after my ordination, she told me I never wrote. She was hurt when I sent a photo of myself to the parish priest but not to the family. "But Mama," I said, "I am not the Pope that there should be pictures of me throughout the village." I showed no gentleness, she said.

She had a hard life—twelve children, great poverty, austerity, never enough. When she was dying, she called for me. I was far away. In Istanbul. I was the Pope's Nuncio. I could not return. My sisters pleaded but I told them I was "like a soldier, under orders." The Church is a demanding mother. She held my letters in her hands as she died, unable to read, hoping to feel the words. I was not there when she died. Nor when she was laid to rest.

But one day I shall see her in paradise—still with my letters in her hands—and I shall try to explain. Even Popes have explanations to make.

I must tell you about the last time I saw her. She had already been dead many years. There was a famous sculptor, Giacomo Manzù, one of the best sculptors in the world. He was doing bronzes of me and brought me some models. "So many Pope Johns," I said when I saw them. "Isn't one enough?" But in one of those bronze models, I saw the face of my mother. It was the first time we had met as Pope and mother. I saw her in the last weeks of my life. And I told her she now had something better than the photo I had not sent.

Manzù was brokenhearted. My face was no longer what it once had been. He saw my face as a crumbling castle, showing the ravages the cancer was causing in my body. He wept, he, a communist that I, the Pope, was not what I had once been. And I, I wept at my mother's face reflected in my own, for the son I had not been to her.

(Return to 1963 and Vatican Office)

I am running overtime again. I spend too much time talking of my father and mother, of my friend Ernesto and my school days. Popes should deal with weightier matters. But I wonder what matters more, doctrine or parents. When one speaks of parents and friends, one speaks a language more universal than that of doctrine. Popes are expected to speak more of God. But, perhaps, one speaks of God whenever the language of our common humanity is uttered.

There is something else I must tell you. It has something to do with war, of what happens to us when the language of our common humanity can no longer be heard.

I was a seminarian, twenty, when I was made a private and obliged to fulfill compulsory military service. It was 1901, before there were world wars. I served in the 73rd infantry division. I got high marks on the rifle range! I'm not proud of that. Six months later I was made a corporal; another six months and I was a sergeant. If promotions came that quickly in the Church I might have been Pope a lot earlier—or not at all.

I was back in uniform, a sergeant again, in 1915 when the world war began. I grew a moustache and was assigned as a hospital orderly.

I was a priest at the time. I hated the war. There, on the battlefields, with the casualties, my *Pacem in Terris*, "Peace on Earth," letter got its start. I worried about my younger brother, Zaverio, who had been called up for service. A cousin had already been killed. I was surrounded by death, by wounds, by blood and curses, by cries in the night, and by questions I could not answer, questions endlessly asked, questions that needed to be raised even though they left us baffled and bewildered. As the century went on, the killing reached horrendous proportions. Soon, it seemed, the century became a valley of death.

I learned something about people in my second tour of military service. The men who surrounded me were simple men. Yet they were often heroic with a nobility I felt was beyond me.

I looked the other day for my wartime diaries. They are lost. But I still retain a page—March 8, 1917.

"There is a young man here, Orazi Domenico. His name will be forgotten. He is nineteen. He is dying. He is a humble peasant with a soul as innocent as an angel's. His intelligent eyes and wonderful smile are visible to me as I write.

"He whispered to me this morning and again this evening. 'I am ready to die,' he told me. 'It is perhaps better to die now because I know I have kept God's commandments. If I die when I am older, the separation will be more painful. It is more painful to leave a wife, children, a home. But now, my dying will break no one's heart. What does it cost me to die now?' "

He asked me to be with him so that he would not be alone when it happened. And I was.

Pius XI kept me on my knees forty-five minutes as a penance. He was clearly angry. Pius XI was the Pope before my predecessor. He was a stern man. And I, I'm afraid, was not an impressive ecclesiastic. You don't send your best men to Bulgaria. And that was where I was. For ten years.

I was there in 1929 when the Depression and the stock market crash unsettled the world. I was twenty-five years a priest in 1929; indeed I was an archbishop at that time. But I felt forgotten, abandoned, frustrated. By 1929 I had been in Bulgaria four years and I seemed to be reaching nobody. My title was more impressive than my future. I had rank but not much influence.

I was the first papal representative to Bulgaria in five centuries. But my career was at a dead end. I did not feel a need to go higher. Just a need to be somewhere else. Ten years is a long time in a man's life. In Bulgaria, it is longer still.

When a priest is twenty-five years ordained, he does a lot of thinking, reflecting. I felt like a bird trying to sing in a thicket of thorns.

God, I know, has a purpose, but the purpose of my time in Bulgaria became clear to me only at the end of my life.

Let me tell you why the Pope scolded me so severely. If he followed his preferences, I'd probably still be in Bulgaria. Then, one day, you might have read, if you cared to read such things, that an old man, a loyal servant of the Church, died in Bulgaria. And neither the man nor the country might have meant much to you. And yet I would have been the same person and Bulgaria the same country. What gives significance to our lives? How are success and failure measured?

But I wander. Old men have the tendency. There is so much I need to say.

Pius XI, Achille Ratti, had been a librarian and was hardly in office as archbishop of Milan when he was elected Pope. I wrote a letter to a Vatican diplomat in Madrid in July 1922, five months after the election. If I find my glasses, I shall read it.

> "The new Holy Father is well. He trusts me. But I try to stay out of his way. I feel shivers run down my spine every time I have to go through those Vatican halls."

I still do.

Pius XI sent me to Bulgaria. What I liked about him, however, was his affection for my bishop, Radini Tedeschi. Few people, perhaps no one else, influenced me more. He was my Pope even though he never became one.

I was twenty-four, a priest a short time, when he was appointed the bishop of Bergamo. Bergamo was the diocese in which I grew up. He made me his priest secretary. It was 1905. Tedeschi was about double my age. Together, we were impressive, if you allow me that vanity.

My own father held me on his shoulders when I was a little boy—to see a parade. But I told you that, didn't I? I repeat it because it matters. He loved me, you see. One does not help a boy see a parade unless he loves him. I used to watch him carefully at night when he came home. Such a hard-working man. I don't know what he would have thought of all this. The Pope lives in a palace. My father would not have known what to do with a palace or a Pope, just as he did not know what to do with his son, Angelo, the Angel.

He would have been as bewildered as I am at the papacy. God has a sense of humor. Jokes become tedious when they go on too long. And so I am dying—of cancer. Hardly elected for the papacy—already marked for death.

Tedeschi was my bishop. I called him that all my life— my bishop. I wrote a book about him, a biography.

Tedeschi was different from me. He was a strong personality, at times a little too severe. A great builder of buildings, energetic—much like my father in this regard. Perhaps the difference between us helped us to become a good team together. Many of the things he did as bishop acted as a guide for me when I was bishop of Rome. I visited a lot of churches and went to hospitals and prisons. People were startled by the pastoral care of their bishop. But I was only doing what Tedeschi showed me a half century earlier.

I was my bishop's secretary three years when we visited Pope Pius X. Pius was fifty years a priest. I carried along 24,000 lire in gold as a gift for the golden anniversary. Bergamo was a poor diocese and we thought the gift impressive. The year was 1908 and the repression against all modern thinkers had begun. Pius was so preoccupied with his campaign and with giving us a speech reminding us of dangers that he neglected to thank us for the gift.

I recalled the incident in my journal even after Pius was canonized, even after I was elected Pope. I do not remember because I wish to nurture the slight. I am surprised at how much a man can get caught up in the zeal of resisting his enemies—so seized by the need that he no longer notices his friends or their gift. When I opened the Second Vatican Council I said that there were no enemies. So many good people! So many gifts! We must thank God for them.

Do I confuse you with the names of so many Popes? There are only four before me in this century. There is Pius X about whom I speak, and Benedict XV who tried to end the great war in Europe and to declare an armistice in the Church's war against its own members. And there was Pius XI who sent me to Bulgaria. And Pius XII who was so impressive that people said I had no right to follow him. I lost whenever I was compared to Pius XII. I had to decide whether I wanted people's approval or my own life. I chose life over applause. It was not always easy.

Popes are more human than people allow them to be. More human than the Popes themselves permit people to see. In me, at last, there is nothing to hide. I am fat and unattractive. No myth here. Just a Pope who eats more than he needs and talks more than he should.

I am happy to talk with you. It gives me peace. And it distracts me from the pain.

Tedeschi should have been Pope. Benedict XV once told me that. Perhaps he is Pope through me since I aspire to be so much of what he was. Tedeschi, my bishop, died at fifty-seven, too young for everything, except that which he had already become. He died fifty years ago. How much he would have liked the Church at this moment of its life!

I learned from him not only how important it is for a bishop to visit the people in his care but also how necessary it is to become involved in social justice. My bishop sent money to a group of workers on strike. That caused an uproar. In 1909, strikers were seen as anarchists, ungrateful, undeserving. That action of Tedeschi inspired me as Pope to write one of my most controversial encyclicals, *Mater et Magistra*.

Radini, you would not have kept me on my knees for forty-five minutes. I must not humiliate others. People who make mistakes suffer enough already.

I had been in Bulgaria five years when King Boris III decided to marry. His choice was Princess Giovanna, daughter of Italy's King Victor Emmanuel III. The Vatican was intensely interested in this marriage for political reasons.

Boris married first in a Catholic ceremony and delighted Pius XI when he promised to raise his children as Roman Catholics. By the time his first child was born, however, Boris had remarried in an Orthodox ceremony and had his daughter baptized in the same Church.

The king told me he could not rule his country as a Roman Catholic, that the Communists were using his Catholicism and allegiance to Rome as weapons against him. Boris believed that his mission in life was to unify his people and that Catholicism made that impossible in Orthodox Bulgaria.

I understood Boris but I worried more about Giovanna.

"Giovanna, Your Highness," I said, "come to Mass privately whenever you wish—here where I live and work. You come here and I shall give you Communion and we shall pray together. Your baby is a joy and I like her name, Maria Luisa. It may be easier if you do not go to a public church where you will be criticized and confronted. Come here and we shall thank God together for your husband and your marriage, your baby and your faith. I know the Pope has said some harsh things about you and the king and the little princess Maria Luisa. You must understand that I am the Pope's representative. And so, I shall protest in his name and mine. But I am also Christ's minister. You cannot be happy with what our Church is now doing, but remember also its better moments. Receive this missal, a special book that I have chosen carefully for you as a gift. And remember our better moments."

Pius XI blamed me for ineptness in the marriage of Boris and Giovanna. And so I did my penance before him, on my knees. Such a contrast! An archbishop on his knees! A child on his father's shoulders! I called both men father. Such a contrast!

In 1934 I was sent to Istanbul. It was a step up the diplomatic ladder. Istanbul is Orthodoxy's Vatican. The appointment prepared me to deal with Eastern and Western Christianity, to become sensitized to ecumenism.

"My dear brothers," I said to the Bulgarians as I left them, "my dear brothers . . . wherever I may go, if a Bulgarian passes by my door, whether it's nighttime or whether he's poor, he will find a candle lighted by my window. You won't be asked if you're Catholic or not. Come in. Two fraternal arms will welcome you and the warm heart of a friend will make it a feast day."

Bulgaria was a success, in my terms, because I learned something about love there. And I think they came to love me. And so, one must decide: When diplomacy loses and love gains, is that a loss?

(Flashback: Simple Office in Turkey)
I arrived in Istanbul in 1935 and remained almost ten years. I was there through most of the Second World War.

Papa, I was there only six months when you died. You died at eighty-one. My physicians tell me I shall die this year—at the age you did. Papa, we never knew each other. It is not only Radini Tedeschi, my bishop, I am anxious to see in heaven. But you. I miss you.

There we shall have time to talk and hearts to understand. Heaven gives us all the time and all the love we need. I shall tell you about the parade you showed me. And I shall not feel like an orphan. The world calls me father though I feel like an orphan.

When you died, I could not get home for the funeral. One did not travel from Istanbul to Sotto il Monte easily in 1935. But I went to the chapel and I cried. I cried so hard I was glad I was alone. I wrote in my journal that I cried that night like a baby, "come un bambino." Like a baby. Wishing we could start over again. And do it better.

Papa, you are dead so many years. I shall be with you soon. And this time we shall watch the parade side by side. I am not only the Pope but your son and I have much to tell you.

The time I was in Istanbul was a sad time for Italy and for the world. My country invaded Abyssinia and a decade of bloodshed brought us through the Second World War. All the mothers of Italy, from Queen Elena herself to those who had hardly enough for food, donated their wedding rings for the war effort. Such a symbol! The surrender of love and life, the giving up of rings, for bombs and bullets and gas.

Things came tumbling down. Papa died. The war began in Abyssinia. Mussolini was in power. Pius XI died. Mama died. The Second World War erupted.

The conclave to elect Pius XI was the longest in this century. The one to elect his successor, Pius XII, was the shortest. At the next conclave, I would be cardinal and Pope.

In 1939, just a month before the Second World War, I met the Nazi government's ambassador to Turkey, Franz von Papen. He was a Catholic aristocrat. I liked him. We got on well together.

The Vatican had misgivings about von Papen. He accepted the Hitler government because he was one of the German aristocrats who believed Hitler was controllable. And they call me naive! In 1934 von Papen gave a speech critical of the Nazis. His secretary who helped him draft the speech was murdered and von Papen became docile. He served Hitler well in Austria, engineering the Anschluss or union of the two countries. He came to Turkey in 1939 where I met him. Turkey was important to Hitler because of its strategic location near the Balkans and Russia. When Hitler proposed von Papen as ambassador to the Holy See, Pius XII said "No" to Hitler. The German bishops had advised him that von Papen was shifty.

The world was now at war.

Von Papen and I got along well. The Vatican considered me naive but relatively harmless. So they let me be.

Von Papen and I had our differences. I disliked politics but I liked people. I learned less from books and ideas than I did from people.

And so I devoted myself to saving lives. Von Papen and I together saved twenty-four thousand Jews. It was, in many ways, the best work of my life. I became, in an alien land, the lost brother Joseph who saved his Jewish brethren from death.

(Return to 1963 and Vatican Office)
So moved was I by von Papen and the courage he showed that later, as Nuncio to France, in my third and last diplomatic appointment, I wrote a letter to the President of the International Tribunal on Nazi war crimes at Nuremberg. I told him I did not wish to interfere in political matters but that Franz von Papen did help me save twenty-four thousand Jewish lives. The letter, I am told, saved his life.

I learned many things in Istanbul. I tried to bring the Orthodox and Catholic Churches together by lowering the wall between them. I did nothing dramatic. Nor did I dismantle the wall entirely. But I did pull out a brick here and there. And since no one resealed the bricks, some good was done.

My last diplomatic mission was to France. I was sixty-three years old. I was appointed in December of 1944 and remained eight years. And then, finally, I was given a pastoral appointment as bishop of Venice, Italy.

I was too unpolished for the French. In France, I dealt with UNESCO and the United Nations. I learned to value people in terms of their good will rather than their religious choices.

Look at me, my friends. Do you see here a diplomat? No! Perhaps an elderly grandfather or an overstuffed uncle. But no diplomat. And yet, in Bulgaria and Turkey and France, I dealt with the hearts of people and nurtured their hopes. The evil people do is most often regretted; the good forever fascinates them.

I lost my parents along the way and may have failed them as a son. They died without my arms and my blessing, without my presence and my words. I made Popes angry and I was dismissed as naive. But I lit candles for Bulgaria and removed walls in Turkey. I stumbled into promotions. And I saved twenty-four thousand Jews.

My brother cardinals, you err—you have made a mistake. I am not an impressive man. You will find me inadequate.

As I saw the votes on my behalf multiply, I asked God to spare me. In my old age, another burden such as this is beyond me.

God would bless me, I believed, if I did nothing to secure my election or to undo it. I waited and watched with anxiety and confusion. I must trust your vote and God's mercy; I do not trust my own resources.

Pius XII, so recently deceased, was a model for all the papacy can be. I am no prince or scholar; I am neither mystic nor diplomat. I remember St. Joseph and I follow his example. When I am told to follow a path, I push my donkey in a new direction and bless the Lord.

What can I give the Church? I have not been a pastor very long. I have been bishop in Venice for only six years. I was not an impressive diplomat in Bulgaria or Turkey or France. And yet you choose me for the most awesome office and the most demanding ministry possible.

I cannot do my work alone. I shall not be Pope in a monarchical manner. I am a priest and a pastor. I shall go to the people and they will sustain me. I am a bishop and your brother. I shall call upon your fraternity and your friendship, indeed upon your patience and forgiveness.

My first request as Pope is that you delay the announcement of this election so that we might have some time together and so that I might gain my composure before I face the world.

I cannot speak to you of theology or plans for the future. But I do wish to say a word to you about my mother and father.

My mother's name was Marianna and she was a good woman. Her name has the name of Mary, Maria, the Mother of Jesus and of Anna, the Mother of Mary—Marianna. I ask for the help of these women tonight—I shall pray to them often in the days ahead.

We learn much from women. When we are babies, they hold us in their bodies and in their arms, at their breasts and near their hearts. They teach us not to be afraid of coming close to another human being. And they make our coming into the world a time of glad tidings. They find room for us in this world, even if it be only a manger or an inn.

I was not able to attend my mother's funeral and so she died, holding the last letter I wrote to her but not holding my hand, keeping in check her tears for the lost, prodigal son she would see no more in this world because he did not return in time. She waited and watched, an advent with no Christmas, expectation without birth, longing and no rejoicing.

When Jesus had his last supper, he filled the room with his friends. And then he passed on to a place where they could not follow. But that night, he talked to them of not leaving them alone and of not wanting them to be servants. And he washed their feet.

This is our last supper room. I must walk alone from it. We shall not be the same after this. You are my friends—not servants. You must not kneel before me. And you will understand if I change the custom of a Pope eating alone. I need company at every meal. I promise I shall behave and that I shall not eat more than the image of my office requires.

My father was a poor man. He had little to give us. In this, the son is like the father. But he did give us life. His name was Giovanni Battista, John the Baptist.

Papa held me on his shoulders when I was young so that I could see a parade.

And so I pray this evening to mama and papa. I cannot get near God without going through them.

I read last evening some words from the fifteenth century Council of Florence, the last formal effort to bring Orthodoxy and Catholicism together. I am an historian as you know.

Cardinal Bessarione had this to say. If I cannot find my glasses, perhaps one of you may read it for me. My hands tremble a bit! Ah! The glasses! And my notes! Now, to quiet my hands.

"What defense will we make before God for being separated from our brothers, when it was to unite us and gather us into one flock that Christ came down from heaven. . . . What defense do we have before posterity?"

My brothers, is the responsibility for the split in Christianity all on the side of the others? Are we to blame in no way? Is pardon only to be given by us? Have we built walls rather than bridges, offered stones when it might have been bread? Do we need to seek forgiveness not only from God but also from those whom we were able to injure only because they were already near us? We cannot forgive without allowing ourselves to be forgiven.

Pius XII died on October 9, a little less than twenty days ago. And we have another Pope. A Pope must not think he is so important. A few days and the Church goes on. I shall remember this in the years God grants me in this office.

Three days before the conclave began, I prayed for the new Pope, close to the place where I celebrated my first Mass in the crypt of St. Peter's. I prayed because Pius XII once said that after him a flood of turmoil would burst upon the Church. Now I know that it is I who must inherit the wind.

God made a bridge from heaven to earth in the cross of Christ. God did not withdraw the bridge when we persecuted his Son, our own Brother.

I would like to remove the wall that separates us not only from our fellow Christians but even from the Communist world. We may not be able to remove all the bricks in the wall. Perhaps a brick here or a brick there may enable us to see the human faces on the other side and to talk to them of peace and of their children. Surely, peace and children move them as they do us.

And then with some of the discarded bricks we might start a bridge. It may not reach to the other side at first but perhaps they might take some bricks also from the wall and begin a bridge from their side. And one day we might join hands. And Christ will be with us. For Jesus is alive in all human friendship and rejoices whenever we become peace-makers and bridge-builders.

I am now to be called "Supreme Pontiff." "Pontiff" means bridge-builder. I am supposed to be the best bridge-builder of all. Help me, my brothers.

The children of this world must not perish in a global conflagration. If the world is destroyed, all our walls will go anyway. Why not take them down now? The children must not suffer from our sins and our walls but they must remember us, their fathers, as holy fathers. In such a memory, we are blessed. A child's blessing is the best blessing.

My brothers, come to see me often in the days ahead. If you do not, I shall not know whether I am proceeding correctly or not. Jesus did not choose one but twelve apostles. I am, at best, the successor of one of them. If I shepherd the Church alone, Jesus will ask me when I meet him where the other eleven were.

And now it is time for the world, not just ourselves. It is time to send up the white smoke—to let others know that we have a Pope. It is time to burn the ballots. There were thirty-eight in my favor. So few votes! Such a difference in the life of a man, in the life of the Church.

The name I choose is John. It is the name most used by Popes in the past. I shall be John XXIII. That title once belonged to a false Pope of the fifteenth century. Since his claim was not recognized, I shall be John XXIII.

Popes who chose the name John did not live long. I am already seventy-seven years old, almost seventy-eight.

I choose "John" because two men who were close to Jesus had the name: John the Baptist and John the Apostle. Brothers, I desire this most of all, that I love Jesus and serve his Church, his people.

Since I have no Pope to depend on, I depend on you.

On my coronation day, when for the first time I am carried on the shoulders of those who bear the sedia or chair I shall remember papa. Pray for him. And pray for me. I shall listen as a Franciscan friar reminds me of my mortality by burning smoking flax before me and observing, "Holy Father, the glory of the world passes away." Most of all, I shall see you and be strengthened.

And now, Your Eminence, Cardinal Canali, you must accompany me to the balcony of St. Peter's so that the world may know we have a Pope. For them, I hope it is good news. For me, it is the most solemn event of my life until the day I die.

It did go well. My first visit with a head of State, the Shah of Iran.

What impressed me more was the visit to Gesu Bambino Hospital. The children there are greviously ill.

The world press was surprised that a Pope would find time in his schedule for such a visit. A pity! People expect the successor of the poor fisherman, Peter, to meet with the Shah and not with the children.

Jesus told us the kingdom of heaven was made up of children. He held a child in his arms as he said this. Not shahs and kings and presidents and prime ministers. Not even Popes. Children.

Viene Qui. Viene Qui, Papa. Come here. Come here, Pope. The children called simply, beautifully. Viene Qui, Papa. I have something to tell you.

Some children were too near death to be impressed with titles and office. Others were too much in touch with life to be awed by someone the world thought important. It felt so good when they held me. A Pope is so deprived of human touching. Viene Qui, Papa. I ran from child to child.

The papacy is not impressive when death is near. I am tonight Angelo, not John XXIII. And I look for Christ to hold me, not as Pope but as one of God's children who is greviously ill.

I did not prove to be the transition Pope they wanted. But I did not live long. There might have been more harmony between the cardinals and me, certainly in the curia, if I did not call the Second Vatican Council. I thought the cardinals would have supported me better. The day I announced the Council to them in private, they never said a word to me. There were seventeen in attendance. They listened politely. I thought they would crowd around, express approval, offer good wishes. They said nothing. Later, one of them, Tisserant, observed that I was not very bright. Another felt it was rash to make such a bold move as calling a Council only three months after being elected. Others were not impressed with ecumenism and reform.

It was precipitous, I guess, to call a Council so soon. But I knew I did not have long to live. And I felt the Church was ill and needed a strong remedy. The Church is not healthy when it depends on its Popes too much. And so I called all the bishops of the world here—all twenty-five hundred of them. Such a lesson for us! The most wonderful moment for the Church in this century came about when the bishops directed the Church and the Pope stayed here in his apartments.

Of all the sins we commit, greed for power is the most frightening. Lust and anger and gluttony are limited by nature itself. Restricted by our very biology.

Power is the papacy's permanent temptation. If Peter who walked with Jesus and beheld the risen Christ could be corrected by Paul, then who am I to believe I always know what to do or to try to give the impression that I am more than I am? A good father learns from his sons and daughters and does not forever pretend he can teach them everything.

Less than sixty years ago, I was a young priest. Just across the piazza, in St. Peter's, I offered my first Mass. I wanted no power then. I want none now. All I wished for was the chance to love God and serve the cause of Christ, to care for people and build up the Church.

It has been a long journey since 1904. Mama. Papa. Radini Tedeschi. Bulgaria. Turkey. France. Venice. My election as Pope is so clear. That night. And the day I opened the Council. And now I wait for death. My next call from God. My bags are packed. My donkey is ready, Lord.

I am back to the beginning. It began with bread and wine in my hands. It is all I wish for at the end. If I know that I have loved God and healed more people than I hurt, then I shall die in peace.

Viene Qui, Papa. How does a child die? If I, as Pope, saved one child's life or helped create a world safe for children . . . that is the power that has no greed in it . . . the power I can possess in peace, the power I wish to have. Not infallibility or universal jurisdiction. I would trade it all if I could be a builder of bridges to freedom for children . . . if I could be a shepherd children call for . . . Viene Qui, Papa . . . I know mine and mine know me . . .

I remember so clearly the first time a Pope invited Communists to the Vatican. It was a visit with the daughter and son-in-law of the leader of the Soviet Union.

Rada, you are Nikita Khrushchev's daughter and you have come to see me, an old man. You do not believe in God as I do but would you accept the blessing of an old man on your children?

Their names. Tell me their names. Something special happens when a mother says the names of her children. No one can say them as she does.

(*Repeating them slowly.*)

Nikita. Alexei. Ivan.

Ivan is John. John is the name of my grandfather and my father. It is now my name. I chose the name myself. When you return home, Rada, give all your children a hug from me but give Ivan a very special one. The others won't mind.

A mother's face is easy to recall. Her voice is always in our ears. And so Nikita and Alexei and Ivan will remember you. I pray that you will be a good mother. I need you to wish with all your heart that I shall be a good Pope, all the way to the end.

You know, Rada, that I have called a great Church assembly—a Council, to see if we can serve the world better. And I have just finished a letter on peace, *Pacem in Terris*, which will be my last major message. If I am a good Pope and my Council succeeds and *Pacem in Terris* is read, perhaps Nikita and Alexei and Ivan will never go to war.

I was moved when I received a letter from a Communist the other day. In it, he said: "I am an atheist and I have learned that you are very sick. Insofar as I can pray, I pray for you. We are all lost sheep until love finds us. And he who brings love is the good shepherd. I pray for you. That you will not leave us so quickly or go away so soon."

Rada, some day you might say a prayer for me. When you do, it will be joined to all the prayers I have said for you. And for Nikita. And Alexei. And Ivan, whom you must not forget to hug in a very special way.

(*Memory of visit is over and scene returns to the present.*)

I learned of the cancer on September 23. Less than a year to live, they told me. Just enough time to open the Council. I would launch this ship but someone else must take it out to sea and bring it home safely. The ship of Peter does not belong to any one Pope. And so we trim the sails. And leave the ship in someone else's hands.

I shall be buried close to where I said my first Mass, in the crypts of St. Peter's Basilica, close to where the Council sessions are held. The debates and the victories, the joy and the celebration, the new life will go on. And I shall not be far from it. From this Council, there will be no turning back. Never again must we do to devoted priests what we did to Chardin and Don Ernesto. The world is filled with God's grandeur. It is not our enemy. There are no enemies.

I must get to the window. Help me into my white cassock. It is not too tight on me anymore, is it?

I want to greet the soldiers who have come to see me. They are in the piazza below because they know the Pope is dying. They have come to celebrate peace, to honor my *Pacem in Terris*, to pray with me.

(*Pope speaks to soldiers from his window.*)

My dear soldiers, people pray that I not have pain but pain is not my enemy. I have memories, undying memories. They fill up my life so that there is no room for pain.

We do not find peace if we rid the world of our enemies. The enemy is the evil that makes us make enemies. When that is overcome, we shall be free.

Last night, I could not sleep. And I prayed all night for children. For you, my sons. For the children you shall have.

You know that I too was once a soldier. I did not make a bad sergeant they tell me.

(*Pope moves back from window and is in the center of room again.*)

I cannot celebrate Mass anymore. A month to live. Not much more.

A month to live. And, then, a new Pope. Viva il Papa.

Out there, the world exalts me but here the Lord rivets me to this bed. This bed must now be my altar. And my love and my dying must be the bread and the wine.

I know God will not reject me. God never turns away the poor.

My life ends but Christ lives and the Church goes on.

Lord, you know all things. You know that I love you. Let all be one, one flock, one shepherd.

Papa, will you lift me on your shoulders in heaven? Mama, I come to see your face again. My Savior, Viene Qui . . . Viene Qui.

I pray for the world I leave, the world that gave me so much love. May there be in this world no night, only dawn and daylight. May no human heart be clutched by evil. May a morning star rise in all human hearts forever.

Lord, you know all things. You know that I love you. I did not make a bad sergeant. Was I a good Pope? Lord, that all be one. You know all things. You know that I love . . .

Discussion Questions

- Can you think of a time when you had a certain amount of "rank" but little "influence"? How did you feel?

- Did you ever feel "like a bird trying to sing in a thicket of thorns"?

- Do you have a favorite Pope? Who? Why?

- Does God have a sense of humor?

- What person(s) do you work well with?

- What first comes to mind when you hear the word "papacy"?

- What are your thoughts regarding the papal elections?

- Can you give an example from your own life when you sought recognition rather than truth?

- Is it true that "the Popes are more human than people allow them to be"?

- Why is it necessary to be involved in social justice?

- What is peace? Is there a price for peace?

- How would you define politics? Should the Church be involved in the political affairs of the world?

- Why do we need to remember the better moments of the Church?

- When diplomacy loses and love gains, is that a loss?

- What is your image of heaven? Whom would you like to meet in heaven? What is the kingdom of God?

- Have you learned more from books or from people?

- What have you "stumbled" into during your life?

- Who are some people you trust? Do you trust yourself? Do you trust God?

- What can you give the Church?

- What have you learned from women?

- What is most important in life? What are your priorities? Why?

- What did God save us from?

- What bold and significant steps do we need to take for peace on earth?

- How do you recognize the nearness of God?

- Why do we need to forgive ourselves? Whom do you need to forgive? Whom do we need to forgive?

- Do the Christian Churches need to come together more?

- Why does Jesus say, "Blessed are the peacemakers"?

- In what circumstances do we need to bridge the gap? What may happen to "bridge-builders"?

- Why is global awareness essential to our faith?

- Do you need to be more independent or dependent of others?

- What is ministry? Are you called to be a minister? Do we all need to be ministered to?

- How do we love Jesus?

Summer Lightning

Act I: Spring
Set: Sacristy
Costume: Alb
Time: 1507

It is not always an easy thing to understand how a life develops or why it turns out as it does. I suppose that if one looks back on the process, one can find lines of continuity. There are connections along the way. But they are not the kind of connections one would have imagined, certainly not the connections one would have chosen had one the freedom to do so.

Patterns emerge that were not part of the original plan and decisions are made which somehow never seem to have been one's own. It is all very perplexing. We probably settle for our lives more than we live them.

The earliest memories I have are the beatings I received from my father. At first they were resented, then expected; finally, I came to believe I deserved them. But you must not think of me as an abused child nor judge my father to have been cruel. He did what he thought was proper. I was not a gentle child. On occasion he asked my forgiveness. At night he prayed at my bedside and helped me to sleep without fear.

A kind father is not easy to come by, on earth or in heaven. I was not more unlucky than most. And so, one does the best he can.

I am a new priest, a young monk, only twenty-three years of age. Wisdom does not come early in life and so I make my judgments with some hesitation.

My father, at least, paid attention to me. I never pleased him but even his displeasure was better than my mother's indifference.

I have never been less able to please my father than I am now. He is here for my first Mass and he is angry. He can no longer beat me but he will find a way to embarrass me in public, even on such an occasion. I expect it. Perhaps I deserve it.

But my mother has not even come.

I wish my father had come here out of love rather than out of fear and anger. Soon after he objected to my becoming a monk, two of my brothers died. He holds me responsible for those deaths. He will make me pay for them. It was bad enough that I would give him no children; it was worse that I even took his.

Somehow he believes that God punished him for refusing to accept my religious vocation. He would understand this well. A punishing parent believes most of all in a punishing God.

What has shocked my father is the notion that his will and God's will could be two different things. What has angered him is the reversal of roles which now allows me to punish him.

And so the beginning of this venture is not very auspicious.

Martin, you are too somber. This is to be a joyous occasion. It is a time for festivity and beer, a moment for exuberant celebration.

I wish my father had a better sense of humor. Being a monk helps one to see the ridiculous more readily. All that one has to do is to look carefully at one's fellow monks to know that God or at least the Church has a love of the absurd.

Monks make wonderful beer and, after a time, look like the casks of beer they create. German monks are more virtuous than their Italian counterparts because they make better beer. German monks are healthy and fat. Italian monks and Popes make wine and love. Wine is for women. The Italians are thin and crafty. Men who drink beer are manly and reliable, belligerent and loyal.

This is not very profound, is it? Well, I told you that wisdom does not come early in life. I learn what I learn. The truth does not have to be justified to be the truth.

Martin, such thoughts at a first Mass!

I never intended to be a priest. In some ways I am not even sure of it now. The whole affair began in mystery. It all started with summer lightning.

It happened less than two years ago. I was to be a lawyer and my father was happy with that decision.

I would have a university education and he had been a miner. He would have me to help support him in his old age.

I was crossing an open field, in July, when the darkness, the wind and the thunder threatened me. It felt as though Satan were sending legions of evil spirits to besiege me. And then the lightning and the fire flashed from the heavens, knocked me to the ground, left me blinded and bewildered. I called out and cried in the rain, "St. Anne, save me. Save me and I shall become a monk."

I don't know why I thought of becoming a monk. It came with the lightning and the fire. I clung to the earth. "Father, don't hit me again. I have not yet recovered from the last beating. God, don't let me die and I shall please you."

Why did I think of becoming a monk? Was it an evil spirit or the voice of God?

I became a monk. It is as simple and as confusing as summer lightning, as clear and as dark as a July rainstorm, as exhilirating and as depressing as the last drink of beer.

I became a monk and I made my promises.

I, Martin Luther, I, Brother Martin, vow to obey. I shall not marry. I shall possess no money. The Lord alone shall be my portion and my inheritance. I shall do what I am told to do for as long as I live. So help me God.

Could all of this have happened without grace?

I was happy at last. I had pleased an angry God and freed myself from my earthly father.

God proved to be more fickle than I expected. I became convinced that God was not really pleased with me but, perhaps, wished only to take another son from my father. I was, you see, the next in line.

I knew I was not good enough to be a monk. But I prayed and I fasted. I followed the rule and I kept my vows. I went to confession with a compulsion and a frequency that satisfied no one. I have been restless and guilty. I never learned how to meet the demands of a father. And God cannot be a mother to us if he wishes to keep his justice. And so God fathers us and rules us. And some of us are orphans from the day we're born.

One day I shall find in the summer sky not lightning but a morning star. One day I shall find on the horizon not the gathering clouds of an angry season but a gentle sunrise and a quiet dawn. One day God shall rain down on me, not wind and thunder but a rainbow of hope. One day I shall live in a world of radiance and all the storms will be stilled. One day I shall find, not justice but love. I shall be blessed, not because I am worthy but merely because I am Martin. One day I shall find mercy in the face of God and God will clothe me with the power and the kingdom and the glory. I shall be saved, one day, when God becomes not a punishing father but a mighty fortress.

Can that day be now?
Who can hasten such a day since I am in need of it?
Who will bring such a God to me?
The monastery and the priesthood have not yet done this.
I long for a better world and a better Martin. But neither comes to me.

Well, it is time to vest for Mass.

(*Martin puts on liturgical vestments as he says these prayers.*)

Cover me with mercy. Cover me with grace. Clothe me in righteousness.

Rein in my vices. Cleanse and clean my heart.

Let my sacrifice please you. Let the power of the priesthood become the glory and the kingdom.

(*Prayers over, Martin says to himself . . .*)

No longer, Martin. Somehow Christ.

I have just burned the papal bull in public. From this day forward, there can be no turning back.

Burning a papal bull in public. Such an action is unheard of in Christendom.

EXSURGE, DOMINE was the title on the document. The title is taken from the first words of the bull, "Rise up, O Lord" *EXSURGE, DOMINE.*

A papal bull . . . a good name for a Roman initiative. The Pope is a bull who has cowed the Church . . . I like that! He has cowed a number of women as well . . . to put it delicately. A papal bull in a Church of china and glass. The Pope has crushed underfoot everything that was not armed against him.

There are other metaphors to fit the occasion. But the company is polite, and I am, after all, a monk and a priest. The papal document from Rome is a lot of bull . . . let me leave it at that. Imagination in an audience is a wonderful thing.

The Pope horns in on the Church. Horns are symbols of sex and the sword. The Pope is a bull in both instances.

And so I burned the bull in public.

The Spanish are better with bulls than we Germans are. We Germans drink beer and charge. We confront the Church and deal with our opponents head to head.

The Spanish dance around their bulls. They use music and capes, costumes and ritual to bewilder the bull. They give us illusion and magic and mystery.

Charles V, the Holy Roman Emperor, the political ruler of all Europe, is a Spaniard. He will dance around the papal bull.

I shall slay the bull and burn the Pope's document in public. I am a German. Let the Italians and the Spaniards drink wine and wobble. We Germans drink beer and bellow.

The papal bull is dead.

So, they are threatening to excommunicate me, are they? Well, let them do their worst. I am young enough to believe they cannot stop me, not yet old enough to be compromised into complacency.

Thirteen years ago I said my first Mass and I wondered then about whether my life would go as I wished. It has not!

The beginnings were not auspicious. But I believed that, perhaps, healing was possible. I do not wish to be a broken vessel in a Church of china and glass.

I want for my life what all of you want from yours. I want it to go right. I want it to make me happy. I want people to applaud me and honor me.

I am not much different from you. I am vulnerable and stubborn, generous and angry, petty and grand, reticent and arrogant, devout and outrageous. Do you not recognize yourself in the description?

I am not the evil man the papal documents depict. Was it fair for Rome to call my mother a dog? Was it right to portray me as an animal?

I admit my language has not always been diplomatic. We Germans are rarely capable of understatement. But you must realize that I am making a protest, the likes of which has never been heard before in Christian history, a protest that depends on me alone.

I am angry at what the Romans have done to the Church of Christ. I am not a bureaucrat or a court official who seeks to keep the system going with diplomacy and tact.

I am the son of a miner. I was not raised as a prince. I did not grow up, as some do today, as the son or nephew of a Pope, someone made a cardinal when he was only thirteen years of age as this Pope was, someone who learns the language and manners of the papal court. Pope Leo was a cardinal at thirteen years of age! He made puberty and the College of Cardinals in the same year.

I act against my own best interests. Do you never do this?

I was not planning to become a priest. I was made a priest, not of my own choosing, and a doctor of theology at as young an age as anyone can recall.

I was docile as a monk. No one expected me to become a reformer. "Brother Martin," they said, "surely Brother Martin, of all people, is not behind this challenge to Rome? Timid Martin. No, you must be mistaken."

It was no mistake. Or was it?

I was a professor of Scripture. How did I become a rebel against Rome? Was it the early beatings or the Holy Spirit, the summer lightning or a call from Christ? Shall I ever know?

What am I doing here, once more, in the middle of a storm? The summer lightning of many years ago ignited the flames which just burned the papal condemnation. The thunder of that July afternoon was in my ears as I hammered the ninety-five theses to the church door in Wittenberg? Was it only three years ago that all this began?

I am not a wealthy man. The language of the poor is more direct.

And I am frightened. I do not have a papal army. I cannot call upon kings and have them defend me. And so my language is not always diplomatic; my thinking is not always nuanced and consistent.

But Rome has no excuses for intemperate language and cruelty.

They wish to burn me at the stake as a heretic. That is enough, is it not, to give one heartburn? No pun intended.

It is not possible to maintain balance when one is being hunted. At the very least, burning upsets one's plans, to say nothing of one's stomach and bowels. These bowels of mine, I would not mind losing those. They have tormented me from my youth. There has been too much tension in my life. I suffer from repression and rage. As a consequence, I retain—more than theology, I am afraid. Constipation affects one's outlook on everything—including the papacy. Enough of this!

And so my language is sometimes beyond all defense. But at least my language is not an excuse for evading theology. I do not only denounce. I also give reasons and remedies. You shall see. I shall share all this with you in a moment.

I am not yet forty years of age and I find myself against an institution that has outlived and outlasted its opponents for centuries. I wonder how much of a future there is for me and my thinking.

I am as perplexed as I was on the day of my first Mass. Then I wondered about the relationship between beer and loyalty; now I speculate about bowels and theology. I seem to be getting worse. Not much future for me in such topics.

Martin Luther can be vulgar and valiant. Judge him not too harshly. He has already been severe enough with himself. Judge him not badly. In some ways, he is all of you.

My life . . . it has always perplexed me. I never know how it will turn out or who is directing it. I worry about myself. I do things I had never envisioned. I still wear the habit of a monk, even though I have denounced Rome. How can I be in revolt against the Church? The Church is the air I breathe. I am a monk and a priest. How can I resist the air I breathe?

I wish my father were here. He was a miner. He learned how to breathe bad air and to go on with his work. He made his way safely out of the bowels of the earth. No matter how deep the darkness, he found the light again. He buried himself in the earth and yet he did not die. He was a survivor and I am a dreamer; he learned to cope and I to rebel.

Why does Martin Luther not have an easier time of it? If I am as talented as my superiors tell me, why have I not gained wisdom? I once thought I was too young for wisdom. Now I know it is too late. I shall never be wise.

And so you cannot have Martin Luther unless you take the foolishness as well. All of it, beer and bowels, cowardice and courage, lust and grace.

Martin Luther will have no easy time with life. And he may never know what made him complicate his life so often.

Julius II was Pope when I was struck by lightning. Julius was more a general than a pastor. He shocked Europe by riding at the head of the papal armies. "Put a sword in my hand," he cried, "not a book. What do I know of books?" He was well named—Julius, more Caesar than Pope.

Julius left a trail of bloodshed and conquest and wounded the papacy in the process.

It was Julius who decided there must be a belligerent basilica, a building over the tomb of St. Peter, a church so massive that people would tremble into insignificance before it. The basilica was to be a political statement. No one would look at it and be able to doubt the power or the permanence of the papacy.

The basilica was to be endowed with the finest art this world would know. Julius brought in Michelangelo, Raphael and Bramante and he made them immortal.

But Christ—where was Christ in all of this? And Peter, the fisherman who wept because he denied his Master? Peter will be crushed by the weight of this basilica as he was by the demands the papacy put on his role in the Church. Peter was a simple disciple, not a prince or a prelate. He was neither imperial nor papal. Peter's shoulders were made for fish nets, not for infallibility and kingship. And his heart was made for Christ.

Peter was to be a shepherd who would care for lost sheep, not someone who carried wood to burn a heretic.

Peter built no basilicas. He brought into the Church of Christ not power or money, only the simple love of a disciple who failed his Master and who needed to be forgiven for this by Christ and by the Church. He was not a Pope . . . he loved Christ too much for that!

Basilicas cost immense sums of money. Julius needed money. Basilicas and Popes are expensive items for a Church to possess.

Leo X, successor to Julius, put indulgences on sale through Europe. He mapped out purgatory as a new land for the Popes to control. Give the Pope money and a soul will be set free. Help the Pope conquer purgatory, now that the Papal States are secure.

The Popes tried to enlist Martin Luther in their schemes but he would not serve. Instead he hammered ninety-five theses to the church door in Wittenberg on October 31, 1517. In the name of the Father and of the Son and of the Holy Spirit.

Martin, still looking for a father. Finding none once again, he tried to invent himself to make himself his own creator. Martin, an orphan once more. No one claims him.

I missed the fire twice. The lightning did not kill me. And Pope Leo's minions who tried to burn me could not find their heretic.

Leo was Abraham looking for a new Isaac but this time the victim was not willing.

And so today it is Martin who lights the flames. And a papal document burns in place of Martin. I rather approve of that substitution. Paper is easier to come by.

When Isaac was saved, Abraham offered a lamb in his place.

If I am not God's lamb, if I am not God's preacher, may the ears of those who hear me be closed so that I have no followers. God's word must consume me. Let me perish if need be but the word of God must not wither on my lips nor the lamb of God suffer in my hands.

No one hears my confession anymore. Someone must tell me I am safe and that I have begun this affair for the sake of our Lord Jesus Christ. If I rescue the Church, who will rescue me?

(Flashback: [Luther now remembers an interview he had with Cardinal Cajetan, two years earlier October 12–14, 1518. Set: office])

Cardinal Cajetan, you are the papal legate. I am grateful you are here. You and I will talk for the next three days. In the year since the ninety-five theses were published, the Reform has gone further than even I anticipated. It is important that you know that. Already more has happened than I intended.

You must speak to the Pope for me. He will not talk to me nor does he answer my letters. He calls no Council though I plead with him to do this. If we have a Council, we shall have no schism, no division, no split in the Church.

Tell him that if all of Europe hears and responds to my summons, then surely more than Luther is the issue. You know yourself that if I am burned, the Reform movement will accelerate. A martyr often makes a cause.

I do not ask that I be vindicated or the Pope vanquished. Let only Christ be victor.

We are both priests. I confess to you that I still tremble at night when I consider what has been unleashed. Am I right, I alone, I ask myself, and so many others wrong? Are the Popes and the theologians, all of them, in error, and you, you alone, Martin, in the right? What if the Pope has Christ with him? What if Satan has deceived me? What if God will no longer hear my prayers and will give me no mercy?

Cardinal, you must know this at the very least. I am as frightened as I am determined, as flexible as I am rigid. I am a mess of contradictions and convictions.

I know where I must go even when I choose not to go there. I do not do as Martin wishes anymore. I am driven either by frenzy or faith; it is often hard to know the difference.

My vow of obedience is still, I believe, intact. I remain submissive but it is now to the word and the Gospel primarily, to the Pope and the bishops secondarily.

I shall stop everything if I can be proven wrong from the Bible. I shall cease if my conscience can be set at rest. I shall become a loyal son if I can only find the right father. I seek the grace of God and the face of God. I need to touch God and know I am not rejected.

I cannot let the Church keep me from the very God and Christ it proclaims. I must be true to myself even if my soul is in peril.

(Second day of the interview with Cajetan.)

Yesterday, Your Eminence, I made my confession to you, so to speak. Today, you wish to hear not the state of Martin's soul but what it is that Brother Martin asks of the Church. Today, you need to hear me speak, not of my fears and doubts but of my program and my plans. Martin is less than the Church. It is the Church which must hold our attention today.

I have written out my proposals so that I might be succinct. I have written so that I shall not be distracted by my personal problems in speaking with you. I have written so that I might be precise. Shall I begin?

(1) I ask that all Christians be acknowledged as priests in a priesthood of all believers.
(2) I ask that the Church be able to call a Council when the Pope refuses.

(3) I ask that priests be allowed to marry, if they choose, since the Pope has no right to demand celibacy when Christ does not.

(4) I ask that each small community of Christians be free to manage their own affairs without excessive Roman interference.

(5) I ask for the free election of all pastors and bishops and their accountability to their communities.

(6) I ask that faith be judged more central than sacraments.

(7) I ask that indulgences be banished and the shameful sale of them forever stopped.

(8) I ask for an end to all teaching about purgatory and the termination of all Masses for the dead.

(9) I ask for a simple ritual in the liturgy or Mass rather than a baroque, court style.

(10) I ask for preaching which impresses and inspires and is central to the worship service.

(11) I ask for the liturgy in the language of the people.

(12) I ask for the singing of hymns at all Masses.

(13) I ask for the full participation of the laity in worship, that they be given the chalice of wine to drink and not only the bread when they come to Mass.

(14) I ask that the Pope live a less ostentatious life style and that the papal diplomatic corps be dismissed.

(15) I ask that the Pope claim no authority over the emperor in the political order and that he reject the title "Vicar of Christ" in the spiritual order.

(16) I ask for the abolition of the Papal States.

(17) I ask that the Gospel be given its rightful place in the Church so that Scripture rather than the papacy might become the norm for Christian belief and behavior.

(18) I ask that Jesus Christ be declared the Head of the Church, its only Savior, its sovereign Lord, its Supreme Shepherd.

(*Third day of the interview with Cajetan.*)

And so, dear Cardinal, we are in our third and final day of discussion.

I do not wish a split in Christianity nor do I favor another Church. I am a Catholic and a monk and a priest and I have chosen to be all three. I petition, as I pledge fidelity to this Church, which has nurtured me and exalted me, that the Church not leave me and disclaim me.

When I hammered the theses to the door of the church last year, I tried to hammer the door closed forever because I was ashamed of it. The door was the entrance to rooms which offered 1,902,202 years and 270 days of indulgences to any Catholic who entered them and viewed with devotion the gaggle of relics and bones, the passel of fingers and toes of saints piously packaged therein.

There were 19,013 particles and pieces of human bodies.

Dear Cardinal, how did we get from Christ to this? Why does the Church of Rome dismember its own people?

The church in Wittenberg had a tooth of St. John Chrysostom in it and straw from the manger Christ was born in; it claimed to have bread left over from the Last Supper, gold from the wise men, twigs from Moses' burning bush.

The Popes would sell the body of Christ if they could find it. They have already sold the body of Christ which is the Church by putting forgiveness on sale all over Europe. I now know why Christ ascended into heaven. It was to get away from the Popes.

When the Pope needed money for the basilica of St. Peter, he sent John Tetzel to raise money here in Germany by selling indulgences. Surely, Your Eminence, Tetzel must have embarrassed you.

He came with streamers and banners, with trumpets and drums. He ran a carnival. The price of admission was guilt and the central ring in the circus was a papal seal.

The seal was not a trained animal, not a papal bull, mind you. It was a seal in wax on an indulgence which promised heaven for the right fee. With your indulgence, Cardinal, I ask you to let me know if you can truly find Christ in all of this.

Christ was a poor man. He had nowhere to lay his head. He did not promise Peter a basilica, only forgiveness. He did not make Peter Pope but a fisher of souls, a shepherd of lost sheep, a brother for those who failed Christ as he once did.

If the Pope has the power to release people from purgatory for money, why does the Pope not empty all of purgatory out of love and not wait for the right price? Is it God who admits us to heaven or the Pope? If the Pope can do all this we need Christ no longer.

A believer cannot sing songs in an alien land. But Tetzel hums his ditty all over Germany:

"As soon as the coin in the coffer rings
A soul from purgatory springs."

Papal seal! Papal *bull!* Even the lyrics are not worth the price. And the theology is worse.

Cardinal, you are an intelligent man. Tetzel is an embarrassment.

I heard the confessions of those who listened to Tetzel. They felt guilty as that charlatan told them they were ungrateful. Why did they let their parents suffer in the flames of purgatory, he preached, when a small sum of money could set them free? What kind of children were they? It mattered not if they were poor; they could always find money for beer. How could they expect mercy from their children or from God when they showed no mercy? If they could show some money, mercy would follow.

St. Anne, save us.

Blessed are the merciful, Christ said, they shall have mercy. Christ put no price tag on mercy.

Even if your mother was indifferent and your father beat you, you wouldn't let them languish in purgatory, Tetzel screamed.

And so, my Cardinal, you have heard all of Martin Luther in these days . . . the doubts and the dreams, the anger and the reasons for it.

You must tell the Pope that I wish to be a son of the Church but I shall not recant. I am ready for the stake if need be but I will not submit. I am driven into the fire even though I once escaped the lightning. Martin, perhaps, was meant for burning. I have come to expect it . . . perhaps, because I deserve it. To die would be less painful than to live with a tormented conscience. Can you understand that, Your Eminence?

(Flashback ends. Return to 1520 and simple room)
If there will be no Council, then I shall become a martyr. Abraham will finally have his Isaac burned after all. Perhaps this is the only way with fathers and sons.

On the day of my first Mass, my father bellowed in public: "Martin, you have not obeyed me. You became a priest against my wishes. Have you not heard the commandment: 'Honor your father'? You became a priest because of the lightning, not out of love. It may have been Satan who brought you to this, Martin. Think of it."

And so I was beaten on the day I was born as a priest. If I am burned at the stake, the bruises will go too. And the Church will be at peace again. The indulgences will be sold without embarrassment and the castle church door in Wittenberg will be free of nails and open once more to the relics.

A great basilica is being built in Rome. And Martin is a passing memory, a nuisance. Rome always wins—not hearts, but at least battles.

Today, I, Martin Luther, burned in public the papal bull.

EXSURGE, DOMINE . . . "Rise up, O Lord . . . A wild boar has invaded your vineyard." That is what the Pope wrote of me.

I am not a wild boar, just a captive to the word of God. Save me, Lord, as you once saved Isaac. Stop the hand of the slayer. Rise up, Lord, and bring me not punishment but the bread of life, not the grapes of bitterness in the vineyard but the wine of your love.

Let me see your face.

No longer Martin. Somehow Christ.

Oh Katie, I love you.

We have been married twenty years, this month, June, 1545.

I was a monk twenty years before I married you. I have now been married as long as I have been a celibate monk. I married you, in June, twenty years, almost to the day, after the summer lightning.

Such a youth! I was only twenty-one years old when I became a monk. I was forty-one years old when I married you. That was not young, but now that I am sixty-one years old it seems to have been.

Katie, you have made me a Christian more deeply than the monastery ever did.

I have been made a disciple of Christ by the word and by a woman. It was a woman who once bore the Word of God in her womb and brought it into our midst as Christ. She, too, was a woman who loved a man in marriage. Mary was wedded to her husband and to the Word. She is both our mother and our sister, someone who nurtured Jesus but stands at our side.

Katie, you have made me husband as well as priest, father as well as pastor. You are that rare person in my life, someone who has not punished me.

I was only thirty-three when I started this commotion with my ninety-five theses. Eight years later, we were married.

It was not a love-at-first-sight relationship. I felt less romantic than obliged when I married you. You were one of the many nuns who had left convents because of my Reform. I felt that I owed you my assistance in getting you into the world again. We seem not to choose our lives but to settle for them. I did not intend that we should have been together for life. I am glad now that we are.

We have created in our home a domestic church even though we could not bring about a Reformed one in Rome. You have had to live with a lot of turbulence. I admire you. It is no easy thing to be Luther's wife. My mother would say the same thing of my father.

The Pope has, at long last, called a Council. It will begin this year, 1545, in December, forty years after the summer lightning, twenty-eight years after the ninety-five theses.

It is too late to heal the split. It will not be the free Council for an improved Church I wanted. It will defend the old order and condemn the new reformers. It will be a papal assembly. I shall not be there.

Charles V, that Spanish rascal, is doing more to get the Council together than the Pope. Popes don't like Councils because they upstage them. But the Spanish know how to dance around the papal bull. Charles has seen to it that the Council will take place in Trent, a city in northern Italy, beyond the boundaries of the Papal States where the Pope could control it better. The Pope did not like this.

Charles will have his Council. But Luther will not be there. The Council, I predict, will do more to divide the Church than to unite it.

We must get used to a broken Church. It will be there for a long time, perhaps forever. Whom will Christ hold responsible for the fractured body of the Church when he comes back in judgment?

Katie, I have so many sins from so long a life.

Did I destroy only what was bad in the Church or have I wounded Christ as well?

Of all my sins, the worst was the slaughter of the peasants. I did not defend them when they appealed to me for help. I told them they could not use my Church Reform for civil reform. I know that they were dealt with oppressively in their daily lives. They had just grievances and unjust princes as their overlords. They saw in my call for a free Church a chance for a free social order as well.

But if the peasants were allowed to have their way in Germany, there would have been no control. Chaos frightens me; I was raised with rigid discipline. I became a monk in a strict community when my life was in disarray. I fear disorder.

The peasants could not keep order. They were not men of learning or administrative skills. How could they win the respect needed to exercise authority?

Each peasant was a victim of an unfair system when seen alone; but, together they became a rabble, a mob, a force as violent and unruly as an untamed storm. They were a flash of summer lightning in a landscape of despair, not made to last, unsettling the order of other people's lives, asking for more than they could handle even if they had a right to more than they received.

They frightened me.

Katie, it was an unhappy dilemma. You have heard me speak of this many times. I knew they needed bread but I could not let them have a sword to get it. If the civil order is shattered, plague and disease, starvation and murder will follow.

And so I asked the princes to stop the peasants, with violence if need be.

And they did.

The very day we were married, Germany flowed with the blood of the peasants.

I had no choice. Church order allows for love and mercy, for freedom and conscience. But the civil order requires law and justice, coercion and authority.

Church order permits options; civil order has no alternatives if the social fabric is to remain intact.

Men may argue about their place in the Church since Christ intended it as a fellowship of equals. Christ wanted neither Popes nor bishops in the Church.

But the civil order was made by God to have rulers and ruled. If this civil hierarchy is not allowed to keep order at all costs, **chaos follows.**

I may have saved Germany by refusing to join the peasants in their rebellion. A rebellion is not a reformation. I may have saved Germany.

But at such a cost! At such a cost!

Katie, this talk wearies you. I speak of politics and you prefer to speak of love. I talk about peasants and you wish to talk of children. I become a theologian when you desire a husband. I am lost in Church structures and you need me to find my place in our family.

But this Peasant Rebellion has poisoned my spirit. Like so much else in my life, it will not be settled. I leave behind me a continent divided and at war with itself, a shattered Church and a fractured nation. Would it have been better had I never been born?

But perhaps it was not all my responsibility. I was an agent of forces straining to be unleased. And yet I did ride the whirlwind and I fanned the flames. I may not be wholly at fault but I cannot be absolutely blameless.

Who sent the lightning? Who sent Tetzel? Who made the papacy? Who printed my books? Who read them? There were conspirators in this enterprise everywhere.

Was I the only sinner in Europe? Or have we all lent a hand in our own destruction?

Give me no justice. I shall perish if I have justice. Give me mercy, dear God. Give me a Savior to stand in my place so that God will not see the sins of Martin Luther.

We need a mighty fortress which never fails even though we often falter.

We require more than we deserve; and, yet, less than this, and we are damned.

This is no fitting talk on an anniversary night. My thoughts before my first Mass were equally inept.

I speak to you, Katie, in such a way because no one hears my confession anymore. The pastor needs someone to look after him, someone to tell him he is forgiven and that peace will follow.

Katie, you were twenty-six when I married you. I am fifteen years your senior. I feel old tonight. I sense that the end of it all is not distant.

My mother and father were present at our wedding celebration. Margaretta and Hans Luther came together. My mother was not at my first Mass but she came for you, Katie.

Katie, you are my morning star. You get up early every morning, before anyone else. You bring me gentle light.

I once stood alone in the world and uttered before emperor and papal legates the bravest and most dreadful words of my life:

"I am bound by the Scriptures . . . my conscience is captive to the word of God. . . . I cannot and I will not retract anything. . . . Here I stand. May God help me."

I wish to tell you tonight that I am bound to you also and my heart is captive to your love. I have never spoken like this to you before but we do not have forever in this life and I must make clear more than theology.

What made you wish to marry Martin Luther? What did you see in him? You must have known he was a marked man and yet you did not hesitate. I do not always understand the selflessness of women with those they love.

Had they burned me as a heretic, you too would have been hunted and hounded.

You gave me acceptance and devotion when other friends and all my enemies sought me for other reasons. But you never tamed my anger in the public forum or my delight in vulgar language.

Katie, you gave birth to six children in eight years. It is a good thing we married late. Had we married younger, the Church called for by Luther would have had only Luther's children in it.

You have learned that Luther burned with more than Church reform.

Summer lightning, morning star. From the fires of fear and violence to the gentle light of a distant star.

Six children—three boys, three girls. Two of the girls are dead.

I think a lot of little Elizabeth. She was born on December 10, seven years to the day after I burned the papal document, *EXSURGE, DOMINE*, in public. She died eight months after birth, in August of the first and only summer of her life. She never lived through autumn.

Two days after her death I wrote to Nicholas Hausmann:

"My baby daughter, little Elizabeth, has died. Grief for her has overwhelmed me. Never before would I have believed that a father's heart could have such tender feelings . . . "

Such tender feelings!

But Magdalena's death makes me want to live no more. She died only three years ago. My morning star has been less bright since then. And death somehow seems less an enemy, more a friend.

Magdalena was thirteen years old. On her death bed, I prayed that God's will be done but I told God how much I loved her and wanted her to stay.

I remember our last words to each other.

"Magdalena, my little girl, you would like to stay with your father here and you would be glad to go to your Father in heaven?"

And she said: "Yes, dear father, as God wills."

And then I held her in my arms until she died. She did not last very long. My arms were not strong enough to keep her alive, only to keep her from being frightened and lonesome as she went away.

I wanted her to know how much she pleased me. It is the least a father can do.

I prayed over her grave:

"Magdalena, you will rise and shine like the stars and the sun. Tell God how much I loved you and prepare a place for me. I shall not be long in coming."

How strange to know she is at peace and all is well and yet to feel such grief, sorrow without end. Katie, I am weary.

Hans, our first child, named after my father, is now nineteen, and Martin is almost fourteen. Paul is twelve and Margaretha, named after mother, is ten.

Children have filled our home, Katie. Not only our children but all those we have taken in. The kingdom of heaven is made up of children, Christ said. If that be so, the kingdom of heaven is here, in our kitchen, every meal.

Now that my theology has abolished purgatory and limbo, there are so many children to care for!

It is my great joy to teach them to sing and to help them learn about God from the catechism I wrote. The Church is at its best when children feel safe in it. Some of the children I have taught may have been sons and daughters of peasants who died in the rebellion. I do not know and I dare not ask. I like to think so.

Germany has more children than ever now. Many monasteries and convents have closed. We have an obligation to the children, do we not, Katie? I teach them not to fear lightning in the summer sky and not to fear the Pope.

But, Katie, it has been a lot of work for you. You tire more often, I notice.

My father was angry at me when I became a priest because it seemed I would give him no children. He lived to see the first three: Hans and Elizabeth and Magdalena. He knew of Elizabeth's death and I understood what he must have suffered when my brothers died. He did not know that I prayed at dying Magdalena's bedside, as once he did at mine. Fathers, even harsh ones, have their gentle moments.

How much I wanted Magdalena to know she pleased me!

I sought a new Church, not a separate or a splintered Church. Perhaps that might have happened if I were less angry and depressed. Even better bowels might have helped.

Papal bulls and papal seals! I lived in a papal zoo. Gaggles of bones and passels of toes! Tetzel's damn ditties and Cajetan's cool logic. Wild boars and living like a hunted animal. Thirteen year old cardinals and a daughter who died at thirteen. Elizabeth never spoke a word before she died and Magdalena speaks to me no more.

Would the Church have remained unbroken if I were more diplomatic? And yet all the moderate reformers before me got nowhere!

I carry a heavy burden of memory and regret.

When I break bread at the Lord's supper, I remember not only Christ but you, Katie, not only the disciples around the table but all my children, especially those who are gone.

I translated the Bible into German so that all could read it and I composed hymns to encourage their singing. I wrote a new liturgy in the language of the people and I sought to make worship a gathering of family and friends.

Did any of the peasants who lost their battle come to pray in the new churches of the Reform?

A heavy burden of memory and regret!

Katie, my morning star, I shall be saved by the word and by a woman.

Such gentle names! Mary who bore the Word and Magdalena who took my heart to heaven with her. Elizabeth who died before I could teach her about God, and Katie, dear Katie, who brought me Christ.

Katie, your body was bread and your love was wine in the wilderness of life. Our bed was a communion table and our table an altar of grace. You made our home a sanctuary; our marriage an act of consecration; our family a community for Christ's presence. In us, ordination and matrimony were wedded. I was a monk in your arms, a priest at your side, a pastor for your life, a Christian through your love.

If Martin is not careful, he will think himself worthy of love. And, then, the anger will die and Europe will be at peace. Rome will rejoice when the wild boar is silent and grapes will grow again in the vineyard of the Lord.

I made less of a difference than I had wished and became a greater danger than I had feared.

Lamb of God, who take away the sins of the world take mine too. Morning star, pray for us. Holy Mary, Mother of God, pray for us sinners now and at the hour of our death. Amen.

Act IV: Winter
    Set: Room From Act Two
Costume: Worn Cassock
    Time: 1546

(Luther's final day of life. It is one year after the time depicted in Act III. It is February. The season is winter.)

And so it is my time also.

I am sixty-two years old.

I die without ever having gained wisdom. Or did wisdom come to me in the knowledge of how little a difference I made?

Through all the seasons of my life I sought the face of God—in the springtime of ordination, and in the autumn of rebellion; in the summer of my marriage and in this winter of my death. I longed for God in all the doubts of my faith as a monk and in all the rage of my protest as a reformer, in all the tenderness of my love for a woman and in all my trust in the word as I die. Saved by the word and by a woman. May it be so.

I shall not live to see the thirtieth anniversary of the Reformation, next year, or the conclusion of the Council of Trent. Good luck, Emperor Charles, with the papal bull. Dance. Do not confront. I have done that already. The bull has been weakened and dancing is in order.

Other people always finish the life we begin and the work we do. Is that wisdom?

I wish Katie were here. Love always lessens the pain. I am far from home and there is not much time left for me.

Little Elizabeth died in August when it was hot and Magdalena died in September when it was still warm. But I die in the cold and frost of February.

I am less frightened of death and even of God because my children are waiting for me. Strange how children shape and change our lives. And papa too. He waits for me. This time he will be pleased with his son. God allows no anger in heaven.

I hope the winter I have brought the Church will blossom into spring, that summer, the season of love, will come again to Christians and God will shine in their hearts and make them flourish.

Heavenly Father, be merciful when I stand before you. Here I stand. May God help me. If only I could have believed in your love, what a son of yours I might have been!

I held Magdalena and kept her company until she died. Since Katie is not here, would you, heavenly Father, hold me a moment? It will not be long. Would you come to my bedside for the last time and pray for me the way papa once did?

If I can have some assurance from you that I am justified, I shall fly to you on angel's wings.

It is not always an easy thing to understand how a life develops or why it turns out as it does. There is wisdom in knowing this too.

Let me not see the fire, only the glory and the power and the kingdom. Not the lightning. "St. Anne, save me and I shall become a monk." Did I break the vow in leaving the monastery? Not a wild boar . . . EXSURGE DOMINE . . . Rise up, O Lord, and be my Savior.

When Isaac did not die, Abraham, his father, must have embraced him with tears of joy and songs of celebration. I would be Isaac a thousand times over if I could find such an Abraham.

Not a wild boar. I was more than that.

Is there no one to hear my prayer? Do not remember the sins of Martin Luther—Martin has a mind of them, every one. I never let a sin go.

All I wanted was a gracious father. Are they so hard to come by?

Cardinal Cajetan, do you have a word in your vocab-

ulary other than "recant"? Am I the only one whose conscience was tormented by all the distortion in the Church's
life?

If only the Pope and I had talked. We had Christ in common and yet that counted for nothing. Was I not worth a hearing? Did not Jesus seek the lost sheep even at the peril of the
ninety-nine who needed him less?

I cannot and will not retract—my conscience is captive to
the word of God.

I can no longer control my life. I am driven into the middle
of the storm, hurled uncomprehending into death.

Saved by the word and by a woman.

Where is Katie, my morning star?

God must not be bartered in the Church for money. God
is the pearl for which we give everything. God is more than
Katie or little Magdalena. God is more than being a monk or
even needing a father's love.

God, let me see your face. Be not asleep tonight. Martin
needs you.

One day I shall find in the summer sky a gentle sunrise
and a quiet dawn, a rainbow of hope in a world of radiance.

Katie, why did you think me worth your love and devotion? Tell God quickly so that I may be forgiven and accepted.

God, let me see your face. I looked for you in every season
and lost you at every turn.

I, Martin Luther, promise poverty, chastity, obedience.

I, Martin Luther, take you Katie Von Bora . . .

I baptize you, Elizabeth, in the name of the Father and of
the Son and of the Holy Ghost.

I am here, Magdalena, almost home . . . don't be frightened . . . can you feel my arms? You will rise and shine like
the stars and the sun . . . there will be no lightning in heaven
. . . nothing to frighten you . . . only peace.

Did I act rightly?

You, merciful Father, mercy one more time. You, mighty fortress, give safety to one more soul.

Holy Mary, Mother of God, pray . . . now . . . at this hour of my death . . . pray for us sinners.

Here I stand. I cannot do otherwise. So, help me, God.

Not a wild boar . . . just a lamb who once lost a shepherd and sought a father's arms.

Discussion Questions

- What are your impressions of Martin Luther?

- How has your life developed? Do you find any "lines of continuity" as you look back on the process of your life? Have any patterns emerged that were not part of your original plan? Did you always intend to be doing the things that you are doing now?

- How do we "settle for our lives" more than we live them?

- What is the difference between being intelligent and being wise?

- How do you image God? Is God a punishing God? If you had to choose one word that best describes God to you, what word would you choose? Have you ever imaged God as a mother?

- Does having a sense of humor have anything to do with the spiritual life? "Being a monk helps one to see the ridiculous more readily." Explain this quote. Does either God or the Church have a "love of the absurd"?

- Define truth. Does truth have to be justified to be the truth? What is the nature of a religious conversion? Have you had a "conversion experience"? What significance does mystery have in your life? How do we tell the difference between "evil spirits" and "the voice of God"?

- When is obedience fruitful? When is it not? Is it ever necessary to break a rule or a vow? How important is loyalty?

- Martin Luther intended to reform the Church, not break away from it. What is significant about this statement?

- How would you describe Luther's inner struggle? Why was Luther searching for the "right Father"?

- Do you have any opponents in life? Who are they? Is it better to go "head to head" with our opponents or to "dance around" them?

- What comes to mind when you hear the word "Church"? How do you define Church? Are we a fragile Church? What are your feelings in regard to the papacy? Does one have the right to judge the Church?

- What issues in life do you rebel against? What, in your estimation, are the most important issues facing our world today? What are the most important issues facing the Church? What do you want from life?

- What can you say about the ambiguity of the human condition? Is life paradoxical? Is faith paradoxical?

- What can be learned from the abuses (indulgences, simony, etc.) found within the Church's history?

- What most struck you about Luther's interview with Cardinal Cajetan?

- Why must one follow one's conscience? Why is it important to develop an informed conscience? What would happen if all people were true to self? Have you ever lived with a "tormented conscience"?

- What do you think of Luther's written proposals to the Church? Which proposal stands out for you? Should the Catholic Church implement all of his proposals today? If not all his proposals, which ones would you want the church to leave aside?

- After experiencing the complete story, what do you now say about Martin Luther?

- What is the significance of the title *Summer Lightning*? What is your favorite season of the year? Why?

- How does Luther view women? What do you think of his description of Mary?

- Is the Church more a Church of the poor (peasants) or a Church of the affluent (bishops and popes)? Which should it be?

- Are confessions important for us? Whom do you confess to?

- What should the nature of authority be in the Church? What is the source of true authority?

- Who is your "morning star"? Why?

- How have you dealt with suffering and death?

- Is there a heaven? How do you image it?

- What, in your view, are the major ramifications of Martin Luther's life on us today? Has the Reformation had a positive or negative influence on Christianity?